New York Sports Quiz

NEW YORK
SPORTS
QUIZ

by
Brenda Alesii
&
Daniel Locche

A Citadel Press Book
Published by Carol Publishing Group

A Citadel Press Book
Published by Carol Publishing Group

Citadel Press is a registered trademark of Carol Communications, Inc.

Editorial Offices: 600 Madison Avenue, New York, N.Y. 10022
Sales & Distribution Offices: 120 Enterprise Avenue, Secaucus, N.J. 07094
In Canada: Musson Book Company, a division of General Publishing Co., Ltd., Don Mills, Ontario.

Queries regarding rights and permission should be addressed to Carol Publishing Group, 120 Enterprise Avenue, Secaucus, N.J. 07094

Carol Publishing Group books are available at special discounts for bulk purchases, for sales promotions, premiums, fund raising, or educational use. Special editions can also be created to specifications. For details, contact Special Sales Department, Carol Publishing Group, 120 Enterprise Avenue, Secaucus, N.J. 07094

Manufactured in the United States of America
10 9 8 7 6 5 4 3 2 1

Library of Congress Cataloging-in-Publication Data

Alesii, Brenda.
New York sports quiz / Brenda Alesii & Daniel Locche.
       p.   cm.
     "A Citadel Press book."
     ISBN 0–8065–1215–6
       1. Sports—New York (N.Y.)—Miscellanea.   I. Locche, Daniel.
  II. Title.
  GV584.5.N4A44   1991   **91–13662**
  796′.09747′1—dc20   **CIP**

Contents

How to Use *New York Sports Quiz*   5

New York Yankees   7

Brooklyn Dodgers   57

New York Giants (Baseball)   71

New York Mets   81

New York Knicks   117

New Jersey Nets   145

New York Rangers   167

New York Islanders   199

New Jersey Devils   223

New York Giants (Football)   245

New York Jets   293

Bibliography   331

Acknowledgments

The production of *New York Sports Quiz* has been an unforgettable experience. As we delved through mountains of research material, we gained a great appreciation of the joys and frustrations associated with each team.

Our goal was to produce a book that reflected the offbeat, fascinating, and intriguing world of New York's major league teams. We think we met that objective, and perhaps exceeded it. We hope you find *Sports Quiz* to be a reference tool, one that embodies the teams' rich histories and storied traditions.

Writing a book of this scope would not have been possible without the support and cooperation of the following:

Professional Football Hall of Fame
National Baseball Hall of Fame and Museum
Naismith Memorial Basketball Hall of Fame
Hockey Hall of Fame
Denny Lynch
Ronald Raccuia, Jr.

Special thanks to a man who believes, Bob Salomon of Carol Publishing, our editor, Al Marill, and a lady who knows her sports, Elaine Chubb.

With much gratitude, we thank Brian Troy, Esq., for his unwavering support.

Photos included in this book have been provided by the following:

Basketball: Naismith Memorial Basketball Hall of Fame
Baseball: National Baseball Hall of Fame and Museum
Football: Professional Football Hall of Fame/NFL Photos
Hockey: Hockey Hall of Fame

How to Use *New York Sports Quiz*

New York Sports Quiz is divided into eleven chapters: the Yankees, Dodgers, baseball Giants, Mets, Knicks, New Jersey Nets, Rangers, Islanders, New Jersey Devils, football Giants, and Jets. Each section contains questions, answers, and "fast facts" pertaining to each team.

For your convenience, the question page always precedes the answer page; questions are grouped separately from their respective answers. (A "Q" indicates a question; an "A" indicates an answer.) Each chapter reflects the chronology of the team. For example, the Mets subheading entitled "The Uniforms" begins with general questions about the players and concludes with the history of those players through the past season.

The questions are current as of January 1991.

As is generally recognized, New York is home to some of the most knowledgeable sports fans in the country. In compiling the hundreds of questions and answers, we may have overlooked some facts and figures. We ask your indulgence.

If you have a particular bit of information to add or would like to discuss the contents of *New York Sports Quiz,* we encourage you to contact us.

New York Yankees

NEW YORK YANKEES

Gehrig, Pennock, Lazzeri, Moore, Ruth, Mills, Meusel, Shawkey, Hoyt, Girard, Paschal, Woods, Shocker, Dugan, Combs, O'Leary, Huggins, Fletcher, Koenig, Reuther, Grabowski, Pipgras, Wera, Gazella, Collins, Bennett, Bengough, Morehart, Thomas, Durst

THE SUITS

Q1 Which managers have the best and worst career won-loss records with the Yankees?

Q2 Of 29 managers, only seven have led the Yankees to world championships. Name them.

Q3 Who is the only man to lead his team to world championships in his first two years as a major league manager?

Q4 Who is the only Yankee manager since 1923 NOT to manage the team in a game at Yankee Stadium?

Q5 Miller Huggins's reign as field marshal of the Yankees ran from 1918 to 1928. What was the team named in his honor?

Q6 In what year did Joe McCarthy begin managing the Yankees?

Q7 Name the manager who wanted to cut Joe DiMaggio's salary by $2,500 after the 1941 season.

Q8 In 1943, manager Joe McCarthy led the AL All-Stars over the NL All-Stars in a 5–3 victory. Besides the game's being the first All-Star night game, what was unique about McCarthy's game plan?

Q9 Joe McCarthy retired as Yankee manager in May 1946. What two men managed the team during the balance of the year?

Q10 How did Charles Dillon Stengel receive the nickname "Casey"?

NEW YORK YANKEES

A1 Best: Dick Howser (1980: 103–59; .636); Worst: Norm Elberfeld (1908: 27–71; .276)

A2 Joe McCarthy (7), Casey Stengel (7), Miller Huggins (3), Ralph Houk (2), Bucky Harris, Billy Martin, and Bob Lemon

A3 Ralph Houk (1961 and 1962)

A4 Bill Virdon (while he was manager, Yankee Stadium was being renovated and the team played at Shea)

A5 The Hugmen

A6 1931 (he would hold his position for 16 years)

A7 Ed Barrow (he wanted to cut his salary because of the war)

A8 McCarthy chose not to play any of the six Yankees on the team. He did this to refute allegations that he padded the team with his own players.

A9 Bill Dickey (57–48) and Johnny Neun (8–6)

A10 He was from Kansas City (or "K.C.")

Q11 In the team's 47th year, Casey Stengel became manager of the Yankees. How many pennants and World Series did New York win in his reign?

Q12 From 1950 to 1960, only two managers led teams to the American League pennant. One of them was Stengel. Who was the other?

Q13 Billy Martin resigned as Yankee manager for the first time on July 24, 1978. Who immediately replaced him behind the bench?

Q14 Bob Lemon is the only manager in American League history to win a pennant after managing a different club earlier in the season. With whom did Lemon start the 1978 season?

Q15 With what seven teams did Billy Martin play during his pro career?

Q16 Billy Martin had five separate tenures as manager of the Yankees. What other four teams did he manage besides the Yanks?

Q17 Gene Michael was named manager on April 26, 1982, succeeding Bob Lemon (who was in his second term at the Yankee helm). Who finished the 1982 season as manager?

Q18 For what three teams did Bucky Dent play during the 1984 season (his last as a player)?

Q19 Stump Merrill, the 29th manager in Yankee history, played six seasons in the minors but never made it to the big leagues. In whose farm system did Merrill play?

Q20 In the 18 seasons that George Steinbrenner has owned the team, the Yankees have had 19 managerial changes (up to the end of the 1990 season). How many of these changes were made during the season?

Q21 On July 30, 1990, George Steinbrenner was banished from baseball. As word spread through the crowd, a Detroit player smacked a home run. Who hit the two-run blast?

Q22 What was the final act of "The Boss" as the Yankee managing general partner?

Q23 When commissioner Fay Vincent ordered George Steinbrenner to relinquish his leadership of the Yankees, who succeeded him as managing general partner?

NEW YORK YANKEES

A11   10 pennants, seven Series

A12   Al Lopez (Lopez managed both the 1954 Indians and the 1959 White Sox—the only other teams to win the league flag in that span)

A13   Dick Howser (Howser managed one game before giving way to Bob Lemon for the rest of the pennant-winning season)

A14   Chicago White Sox (he left the White Sox on June 30, 1978)

A15   New York (1950–57), Kansas City (1957), Cleveland (1959), Detroit (1958), Cincinnati (1960), Minnesota and Milwaukee (1961)

A16   Minnesota Twins, Detroit Tigers, Texas Rangers, and Oakland A's

A17   Clyde King (King was later replaced in the off-season by Billy Martin. It was Martin's third term as manager)

A18   Texas Rangers (who released him just prior to the season), Yankees (who signed him on June 7 and released him on July 9), and Kansas City (who signed him on August 16 and released him on October 10)

A19   Philadelphia Phillies (as a catcher)

A20   10 (1975, 1978, 1979, 1981, 1982 [2], 1985, 1988, 1989, 1990)

A21   Cecil Fielder (New York won the game, 6–2)

A22   He named Gene Michael as general manager (replacing Pete Peterson)

A23   Broadway producer Robert Nederlander

Q24 In what city did the Yankee team originate?

Q25 The Yankees were the first team to retire a player's number. Who was the first man so honored?

Q26 What pitcher holds the all-time record for career wins against the Yankees?

Q27 In 1903, the Baltimore franchise was moved to New York and the Highlanders were born. When was the team name changed to "Yankees"?

Q28 The first contest between the Yankees and Red Sox took place on May 7, 1903. Who won the game?

Q29 What four parks have the Yankees called home?

Q30 How many seasons have the Yankees led the league in home runs?

Q31 In what year did the Yankees win their first pennant?

Q32 Yankee Stadium sits on land formerly owned by what famous millionaire?

Q33 What was the visiting team in the first game at Yankee Stadium on April 18, 1923?

Q34 "The House That Ruth Built" was opened in 1923. Who hit the first World Series home run in the park?

Q35 The 1927 Yankees are acknowledged as the greatest team to play the game. What club languished in second place, 19 games behind the pennant winners?

NEW YORK YANKEES

A24   Baltimore (Frank Farrell and Bill Devery bought the club for $18,000 and moved the team to New York in 1903)

A25   No. 4, Lou Gehrig (1939)

A26   Walter Johnson (he defeated New York 60 times during his career)

A27   10 years later (1913)

A28   The Red Sox (6–2 in Boston)

A29   Hilltop Park (or American League Park, as it was commonly called in New York), the Polo Grounds, Yankee Stadium, and, while renovations were being made to Yankee Stadium in 1974/75, Shea Stadium

A30   34 seasons (the first time was in 1915 with 31 team homers)

A31   1921 (their 19th season; they beat out second-place Cleveland by 4½ games, but lost the first Subway Series to the Giants)

A32   William Waldorf Astor

A33   Boston Red Sox (Yankees won, 4–1)

A34   Giant Casey Stengel

A35   Philadelphia Athletics

Q36 1928 was a carbon copy of the previous season, as the Yankees won both the league and most of the hitting categories again. The only blemish on the season was when they were beaten 24 to 6—the most runs given up by the Bombers. Name the team that defeated the Yanks.

Q37 Though they finished third in the standings, the 1930 team was one of the most potent hitting clubs in baseball history. Its .309 team batting average is a club record. How many Yankees batted .300 or better?

Q38 What opposing pitcher threw the first no-hitter against New York in Yankee Stadium?

Q39 Who is the only man to have pitched to both Babe Ruth and Mickey Mantle in regular season major league games?

Q40 In 1954, the Yankees had a 103–51 record, but had to settle for second place. Who edged them out that year?

Q41 There were two pine tar incidents with the Yankees—once in 1975 and again in 1983. Name the batters involved and explain the league ruling.

Q42 Name the AL official who ruled on the 1983 pine-tar incident.

Q43 When Jim Deshaies took the mound for New York on August 7, 1984, what milestone did he mark?

Q44 A ''putout'' by Dave Winfield once cost him a $500 bond in Toronto. Why were civil charges brought against Winfield in the 1983 game?

Q45 This former Yankee was the 5,000th career strikeout for Nolan Ryan. Name him.

Q46 There are 21 monuments and plaques in Yankee Stadium's Monument Park. Two are dedicated to people not associated with baseball. Whom do they honor?

NEW YORK YANKEES

A36   Cleveland Indians (July 29, 1928)

A37   Nine

A38   Cleveland's Bob Feller (April 30, 1951)

A39   Al Benton (Philadelphia: 1934–35; Detroit: 1938–48; Cleveland: 1949–50; and Boston: 1952)

A40   Cleveland Indians (111–43)

A41   In 1975, the Minnesota Twins appealed a home run hit by Thurman Munson. Munson was called out and the homer was disallowed. In 1983, manager Martin appealed a two-run homer that Royal George Brett hit. After the Yankees won the appeal, the decision was reversed by the AL president.

A42   Lee McPhail (the Royals won the game, 4–3)

A43   He became the 1,000th player to appear in a game as a Yankee

A44   As Winfield was warming up between innings, he threw a ball at a seagull that had landed near him. The ball struck and killed the bird. Canadian authorites pressed charges against him for cruelty to animals (but the charges were later dropped.)

A45   Rickey Henderson (August 22, 1989)

A46   Pope Paul VI and Pope John Paul II (the plaques commemorate the masses the pontiffs held at the stadium in 1965 and 1979 respectively)

Q47 What Yankee holds the highest single-season winning percentage for pitchers with 20 or more wins?

Q48 Who is the only hurler to win 20 games without 200 innings pitched?

Q49 What Yankee registered two no-hitters in the same season?

Q50 Who pitched the first nine-inning no-hitter for New York?

Q51 What record does pitcher Vic Raschi hold?

Q52 What pitcher has registered the most saves in a Yankee uniform?

Q53 Who is the only Yankee pitcher to win the American League MVP Award?

Q54 New York's worst winning percentage was registered in 1912, when the team went 50–102 for a .329 average. The all-time team low for shutouts was set that year with three, and one pitcher was responsible for all of them. Name him.

Q55 George Mogridge became the first Yankee southpaw to throw a no-hitter. It happened against the Red Sox at Boston on April 24, 1917 (NY won, 2–1). What former Yankee was the next lefty to accomplish this feat?

Q56 What Boston Red Sox pitcher has the best career winning percentage against the Yankees (minimum: 20 decisions)?

Q57 On August 16, 1920, Cleveland Indian Ray Chapman was killed by a pitch. What Yankee pitcher became infamous for his role in the tragedy?

Q58 Who was the only 20-game winner on the '27 Yankees?

Q59 What Yankee was the last pitcher to face Ty Cobb in a major league game (September 11, 1928)?

NEW YORK YANKEES

A47   Ron Guidry (1978: 25–3; .893)

A48   Bob Grim (1954: W 20, L 6; .326 ERA; 199 IP)

A49   Allie Reynolds (against Cleveland and against Boston, 1951)

A50   Thomas Hughes (August 10, 1910; Hughes lost the game in 11 innings against Cleveland, 5–0)

A51   Most balks in a single game (four)

A52   Dave Righetti

A53   Spud Chandler (1943)

A54   Russell Ford

A55   Dave Righetti (1983)

A56   Babe Ruth (17–5)

A57   Carl Mays

A58   Waite Hoyt (22–7, with an ERA of 2.63)

A59   Henry Johnson (Cobb popped out to SS Mark Koenig)

Q60 This pitcher was traded to New York by Boston in 1929. He went on to average 16 wins per season for the next 13 years. Name him.

Q61 What Yankee threw the first pitch and won the first All-Star Game?

Q62 Allie Reynolds's second no-hitter on the 1951 season came against the Red Sox. Who made the last out for Boston?

Q63 What one-time Yankee gave up the first home run of Hank Aaron's major league career on April 23, 1954?

Q64 What New York pitcher was the first American League Cy Young Award winner?

Q65 What former Yankee won a game against a pitcher who threw 12 perfect innings (May 26, 1959)?

Q66 Name the Yankee who was the last pitcher to hit an inside-the-park grand slam home run.

Q67 What pitcher won the AL Rookie of the Year Award in 1968 with a 17–12 record and 2.05 ERA?

Q68 This Yankee was the last pitcher to get a regular-season hit prior to the implementation of the DH rule. Who was he?

Q69 Name the pitcher who gave up the first home run to a designated hitter.

Q70 In 1978, Ron Guidry was the unanimous choice for the Cy Young Award. Who are the only other AL pitchers to be accorded such an honor?

Q71 Gaylord Perry, a Yankee in 1980, was involved in the first consecutive no-hitters pitched in a series between two clubs. Name the opposing teams and the pitcher who threw the second no-hitter.

Q72 What pitcher paced the 1981 American League pennant champs with just 11 wins?

Q73 Who threw the next Yankee no-hitter after Don Larsen pitched his perfect game in the 1956 Series?

NEW YORK YANKEES

A60   Red Ruffing

A61   Lefty Gomez

A62   Ted Williams (he fouled to Yogi Berra twice—the first time Berra dropped the ball)

A63   Vic Raschi (while playing for the St. Louis Cardinals)

A64   Bob Turley (1958)

A65   Lew Burdette (While with the Milwaukee Braves, Burdette completed a 13-inning game in which Pirate Harvey Haddix pitched 12 perfect innings. In the 13th, with the score 0–0, an error, a walk, and a hit resulted in a 1–0 score and a one-hit loss for Haddix. Burdette threw a 12-hit shutout.)

A66   Mel Stottlemyre (July 20, 1965: against Boston)

A67   Stan Bahnsen (1966, 1968–71)

A68   Larry Gowell (in his only at-bat in the majors, Gowell hit a third-inning double off Milwaukee's Jim Lonborg, October 4, 1972)

A69   Sparky Lyle (April 8, 1973: to Red Sox DH Orlando Cepeda)

A70   Detroit's Denny McLain (1968) and Boston's Roger Clemens (1986)

A71   On September 17, 1968, Perry threw a 1–0 no-hitter for the Giants against St. Louis, while Cardinal Ray Washburn won a 2–0 no-hitter the next day against San Francisco

A72   Ron Guidry (11–5)

A73   Dave Righetti (July 4, 1983: against Boston)

Q74 Joe Niekro hit only one home run in his entire career. Who served up the pitch?

Q75 The first time a pitcher started and played a game as a designated hitter occurred on June 11, 1988. Name the Yankee hurler. (Hint: He played only two seasons with the club, 1987–1988.)

Q76 On July 1, 1990, Andy Hawkins threw a no-hitter against the White Sox, but lost 4–0 thanks to three eighth-inning errors. Name the trio of players responsible for the errors.

Q77 Who was the last pitcher before Hawkins to throw a complete-game no-hitter and lose?

Q78 Andy Hawkins's no-hitter came on the heels of two other no-hitters; both were thrown on June 29, 1990—the first time two no-hitters were pitched on the same day in different leagues. Name the two hurlers.

Q79 Three Yankees have hit two home runs in one inning. In 1977, Thurman Munson did it in his ninth season with the team, while the other two players were in their rookie years. Who were these first-year Yankees?

Q80 The major league single-season 50-home-run plateau has been reached on 18 occasions. How many times has a Yankee achieved it?

Q81 Who is the last Yankee to hit for the cycle?

Q82 Who is the only player to rack up over 400 total bases five times in his career?

Q83 Two Yankees have won the American League MVP award three times. Who were they?

Q84 Three Yankees have won the American League MVP in consecutive years. Name them.

Q85 Who scored the first ever Yankee run in 1903?

Q86 What three Hall-of-Famers played for the Yankees in their inaugural season, 1903?

NEW YORK YANKEES

A74 His brother, Phil (Astro Joe hit Atlanta Brave Phil and also outpitched him in a 4–3 victory)

A75 Rick Rhoden

A76 Mike Blowers (who bobbled a grounder at third for a two-out error), Jim Leyritz (who dropped a fly ball while the bases were loaded, allowing three runs to score), and Jesse Barfield (who dropped a fly ball to allow one run to score). Between Blowers's and Leyritz's errors, Hawkins loaded the bases with three consecutive walks.

A77 Houston Colt .45s' Ken Johnson (April 23, 1967: lost to Cincinnati 1–0)

A78 Oakland's Dave Stewart and L.A.'s Fernando Valenzuela (they each won their game)

A79 Joe DiMaggio (1936) and Joe Pepitone (1962)

A80 Seven times (Babe Ruth—four times; Mickey Mantle—twice; Roger Maris)

A81 Bobby Murcer—August 29, 1972 (13 Yankees have hit for the cycle)

A82 Lou Gehrig

A83 Joe DiMaggio (1939, 1941, 1947) and Yogi Berra (1951, 1954, 1955)

A84 Yogi Berra (1954 and 1955), Mickey Mantle (1956 and 1957), and Roger Maris (1960 and 1961)

A85 "Wee Willie" Keeler (April 22, 1903, at Washington in the first inning. New York lost the game, 3–1)

A86 Clark Griffith, William Henry "Wee Willie" Keeler, and Jack Chesbro

Q87   Who is the only player to hit in the All-Star games played at Yankee Stadium, the Polo Grounds, and Ebbets Field?

Q88   Who is the first Yankee to lead the American League in batting?

Q89   Which Yankee became the first player selected as an All-Star starter in each of his first three full seasons in the big leagues?

Q90   The first official team captain was Roger Peckinpaugh in 1914. What other position did he assume that year?

Q91   This Yankee is one of two players to hit for the cycle three times. Name him.

Q92   Who comprised "Murderer's Row"?

Q93   In 1931, Lou Gehrig and Babe Ruth tied for the home run crown. How many did each have?

Q94   Six Yankees were named to the first All-Star team in 1933. Name them.

Q95   What Yankee committed the first error in All-Star competition?

Q96   What Yankee outfielder was the first AL batter in the first All-Star Game (July 6, 1933)?

Q97   The 1936 Yankees had five players with more than 100 RBIs each. Name the quintet.

Q98   Boston's Ted Williams won the Triple Crown twice—1942 and 1947—but failed to capture the American League MVP award either year. Name the Yankees who edged him out for the honor in 1942 and 1947.

Q99   Name the 1944 Yankee first baseman who led the American League in home runs with only 22.

Q100   What position did Yogi Berra want to play when he came to the Yankees in 1946?

Q101   On two separate occasions—1941 and 1947—the Yankees had three players who hit 30 or more home runs. Name the players. (Hint: There are no repeat hitters.)

NEW YORK YANKEES

A87   Joe DiMaggio

A88   Babe Ruth (1924)

A89   Joe DiMaggio

A90   Manager (he split the managerial duties with Frank Chance)

A91   Bob Meusel—1921, 1922, 1928 (he is tied with Brooklyn Dodger Babe Herman)

A92   Babe Ruth, Lou Gehrig, Bob Meusel, Tony Lazzeri, Earle Combs, Joe Dugan, and Mark Koenig (at times, the name referred to the entire team)

A93   46 home runs

A94   Ben Chapman, Bill Dickey, Lou Gehrig, Lefty Gomez, Tony Lazzeri, and Babe Ruth

A95   Lou Gehrig (July 6, 1933: Gehrig dropped a fly ball in the fifth inning)

A96   Ben Chapman (in the first meeting of the two leagues, Chapman grounded out to Cardinal Pepper Martin)

A97   Lou Gehrig (152), Joe DiMaggio (125), Tony Lazzeri (109), Bill Dickey (107), and George Selkirk (107)

A98   1942: Joe Gordon; 1947: Joe DiMaggio

A99   Nick Etten

A100   Shortstop

A101   1941: Charlie Keller (33), Tommy Henrich (31), Joe DiMaggio (30); 1947: Johnny Mize (51), Willard Marshall (36), Walker Cooper (35)

Q102 Cliff Mapes played in the majors from 1948 to 1952, hit 38 home runs, and compiled a .242 career batting average, but his significance in baseball history lies in another area. For what is Mapes known?

Q103 Three Yankees were named AL Rookie of the Year during the 1950s. Name them.

Q104 What two players from New York City won American League and National League Rookie of the Year honors in 1951?

Q105 In what year did Elston Howard become the first black player to wear the Yankee pinstripes?

Q106 Phil Rizzuto played two positions in his 13-year career with the Yankees. He started 1,647 games at shortstop and two games at another position. Where was he for the pair of games?

Q107 Cleveland's Herb Score was touted as the next Bob Feller, but his career was cut short when a line drive caught him in the face. Who was the Yankee batter on that play?

Q108 In the 1960 American League expansion draft, the Los Angeles Angels and the Washington Senators both selected pitchers from the Yankee roster. Name the two players.

Q109 What pitcher gave up Roger Maris's 60th home run, allowing him to tie the Babe's record and eventually surpass it?

Q110 Prior to Don Mattingly in 1985, who was the last Yankee to lead the American League in RBIs?

Q111 Who had the higher batting average: Babe Ruth, the year in which he hit 60 home runs, or Roger Maris, when he slammed 61?

Q112 In 1961, Roger Maris hit 61 home runs. How many times was he intentionally walked that year?

Q113 Name the baseball commissioner who required that an asterisk be placed next to Maris's name in the record books after he hit 61 homers.

Q114 Who was the last second baseman before Steve Sax to get 200-plus hits for the Yankees?

NEW YORK YANKEES

A102 He wore No. 3 for the Yankees before New York retired the number in honor of Babe Ruth, and donned No. 7 immediately before Mickey Mantle joined the team

A103 Gil McDougald (1951), Bob Grim (1954), and Tony Kubek (1957)

A104 NL: Giants' Willie Mays; AL: Yankees' Gil McDougald (McDougald won the Baseball Writers' Association award while Chicago's Minnie Minoso took *The Sporting News's* citation. 1951 was also Mickey Mantle's rookie year)

A105 1955

A106 Second base

A107 Gil McDougald

A108 Angels: Eli Grba; Senators: Bobby Shantz (Grba played with the Yanks 1959–61, and Shantz was with the team 1957–60)

A109 Baltimore's Jack Fisher (September 26, 1961)

A110 Roger Maris (1961; Maris led the league in 1960 and 1961 with 112 and 142 RBIs respectively)

A111 Ruth (the Bambino hit .356 in 1927 against Maris's .269 in 1961)

A112 None (with Mantle batting after him, pitchers elected to go through Maris rather than around him)

A113 Ford Frick (the asterisk indicates that the 1961 record was achieved in a 162-game season rather than a season of 154 games, as in 1927)

A114 Bobby Richardson (1962: 209) (The only other Yankee second baseman to get 200-plus hits is Snuffy Stirnweiss—1944: 205)

Q115 With what four teams did Roger Maris play major league ball?

Q116 The longest game in Yankee history was a seven-hour, 22-inning contest against the Tigers on June 24, 1962. What outfielder hit his only major league home run to win the game for New York, 9–7?

Q117 Name the Red Sox pitcher who gave up Roger Maris's 61st home run.

Q118 On December 8, 1966, the Yankees traded Roger Maris to the St. Louis Cardinals. Whom did they receive in return?

Q119 With the retirement of No. 8 in 1972, two players were honored at the same time. Who were the players?

Q120 Next to the Babe Ruth trade, this deal may have been the most one-sided between New York and Boston. Who was sent to the Red Sox in exchange for Sparky Lyle in 1972?

Q121 Two Yankees were in the news in 1973 for their off-the-field activities. Name the two who gained notoriety for swapping their wives.

Q122 Who hit the last home run in the old Yankee Stadium in September 1973?

Q123 The first designated hitter to play in the majors was a Yankee in a game against Boston on April 5, 1973. Who was he?

Q124 The "heir apparent" to Mickey Mantle, Bobby Murcer, had three separate terms in New York (1965–66, 1969–74, and 1979–83). For whom was he traded prior to the 1975 season?

Q125 What former Yankee scored the 1,000,000th run in baseball while playing for the Houston Astros in 1975?

Q126 What three players stole 30-plus bases each in the same season?

Q127 Thurman Munson was named the team's fifth captain in 1976. What player did he succeed in that capacity?

Q128 For what two teams had Reggie Jackson played before arriving in New York as a free agent in 1976?

NEW YORK YANKEES

A115 Cleveland Indians, Kansas City A's, Yankees, and St. Louis Cardinals

A116 Jack Reed (Reed played three years and 222 games in the majors, all with New York)

A117 Tracy Stallard

A118 Charley Smith (1967–68)

A119 Catchers Bill Dickey and Yogi Berra

A120 Danny Cater and Mario Guerrero

A121 Mike Kekich and Fritz Peterson

A122 Duke Sims of the Yanks

A123 Ron Blomberg (he walked on five ptiches)

A124 San Francisco's Bobby Bonds (Bonds lasted one season with the club)

A125 Bob Watson

A126 Mickey Rivers (43), Willie Randolph (37), and Roy White (31) (1976)

A127 Lou Gehrig (the Yanks never had a captain between 1941 and 1976)

A128 Baltimore Orioles and Oakland A's

Q4. Who is the only Yankee manager since 1923 NOT to manage the team in a game at Yankee Stadium?

NEW YORK YANKEES

Q9. Joe McCarthy retired as Yankee manager in May 1946. This player and another Yank managed the team during the balance of the year. Who were they?

Q63. What one-time Yankee gave up the first home run of Hank Aaron's major league career on April 23, 1954?

Q250. Name the Yank who replaced the injured Willie Randolph at second base in the 1978 Series.

Q129 What player was acquired by New York in 1977 in exchange for Oscar Gamble, Bob Polinsky, Dewey Hoyt, and cash?

Q130 Until 1978, when Jim Rice accomplished it, who was the last American League player to gain over 400 total bases?

Q131 Thurman Munson died in an airplane crash on August 2, 1979. On the evening of his funeral, the Yankees defeated the Orioles, 5–4, with all of New York's runs knocked in by one player. Who had the five RBIs?

Q132 Who has the dubious distinction of being the first player to hit into a Yankee triple play?

Q133 How many times did Reggie Jackson win or tie for the American League home run championship?

Q134 Since Roger Maris led the American League with 61 home runs in 1961, only two Yankees have been home run champs in the past 30 years. Who are they?

Q135 The Yankees have a number of players who have finished first and second for the league batting title. Who are the last two players to finish in that order in the same year?

Q136 After the 1981 season, Reggie Jackson was granted free agency and soon signed with the California Angels. On September 17, 1984, he hit his 500th home run (becoming the 13th player to do so). Who served up the pitch?

Q137 Rickey Henderson won nine stolen base titles from 1980 to 1989. Who is the only other player to win the title in that decade?

Q138 What number did Rickey Henderson wear with the Yankees, and why did he select that number?

Q139 On April 20, 1988, the Yankees registered their 10,000th team home run. Who hit it?

Q140 Don Mattingly led the team in hits from 1984–88. Who are the only other two players to lead the Yanks for five straight years?

Q141 "Prime Time" was a first-round pick of the Atlanta Falcons, but his value was considerably less in the baseball draft. In what round was Deion Sanders selected by the Yankees in the 1988 free agent draft?

NEW YORK YANKEES

A129 Russell "Bucky" Dent (from the Chicago White Sox)

A130 Joe DiMaggio (1937: 418)

A131 Bobby Murcer (Murcer delivered Munson's eulogy earlier in the day)

A132 Damaso Garcia—September 21, 1979 (at Toronto)

A133 Four times (Oakland: 1973 and 1975; New York: 1980; California: 1982)

A134 Graig Nettles (1976: 32 HRs) and Reggie Jackson (1980: 41 HRs)

A135 Don Mattingly (.343) and Dave Winfield (.340) in 1984

A136 Kansas City's Bud Black

A137 Seattle's Harold Reynolds (1987: 60 stolen bases; Henderson had 41 that season)

A138 No. 24; because it was the number of his idol, Willie Mays

A139 Claudell Washington (off Minnesota's Jeff Reardon at the Metrodome)

A140 Mickey Mantle (1955–59) and Lou Gehrig (1930–34)

A141 30th round

THE UNIFORMS

Q142 Jack Clark was not the savior the Yankees, or their fans, expected, so the club traded him after a single season in New York. To what team was he sent in 1988?

Q143 On June 21, 1989, Rickey Henderson was traded. Who moved into his lead-off spot and responded with a three-for-five batting day against the Chicago White Sox?

Q144 In 1988, Don Mattingly became the sixth Yankee to hit .300 or better in six straight seasons (the last time was 1942). Who were the other five?

Q145 Whom did New York send to Seattle for Steve Balboni?

Q146 Dave Winfield was drafted twice in the baseball free agent draft, once in the NFL draft, and twice by basketball teams—one NBA and the other ABA. Name the five teams that vied for Winfield's services.

Q147 On July 22, 1989, the Yankees sent Mike Pagliarulo and Don Schulze to the Padres for two pitchers. Name the new Yankees.

Q148 How many separate tours of duty has Rick Cerone seen with the Yankees?

Q149 Match the player with his real first name(s):

(1) Alfred Manuel	(a) Lefty Gomez
(2) Vernon	(b) Yogi Berra
(3) Charles Dillon	(c) Whitey Ford
(4) Lawrence Peter	(d) Casey Stengel
(5) Edward	(e) Billy Martin

—THE BABE—

Q150 Hank Aaron surpassed Babe Ruth as the all-time home run leader. Whose record did Ruth shatter?

Q151 What pitcher gave up more home runs to Ruth in his career than any other hurler?

Q152 Babe Ruth is the only player to hit grand slams in consecutive games more than once. How many times did he do that?

NEW YORK YANKEES

A142 San Diego (with Pat Clements, for Lance McCullers, Jimmy Jones, and Stanley Jefferson)

A143 Steve Sax (the Yanks lost the game, 7–3)

A144 Earle Combs, Bill Dickey, Lou Gehrig, Babe Ruth, and Joe DiMaggio (DiMaggio was the last to accomplish it)

A145 Dana Ridenour

A146 Baseball: 1969 Orioles and 1973 Padres (signed with Padres); NFL: 1973 Minnesota Vikings; NBA: 1973 Atlanta Hawks; ABA: 1973 Utah Stars

A147 Walt Terrell and Fred Toliver (Toliver was the "player to be named later" in the deal)

A148 Three (1980: acquired from Toronto; 1984: traded to Atlanta; 1987: signed as a free agent and released in 1988; 1990: signed as free agent)

A149 1—e; 2—a; 3—d; 4—b; 5—c

_____ · _____

A150 Roger Connor (Connor, who played for a number of teams, held the record of 137 career home runs until Ruth passed him in 1921)

A151 Rube Walberg (1923–37; gave up 18 home runs while pitching for the Red Sox and Philadelphia Athletics)

A152 Twice (September 27 and 29, 1927, and August 6 and 8, 1929)

Q153 In Ruth's first season in New York, he set an all-time slugging record that may never be beaten. What is it?

Q154 Babe Ruth had two three-homer Series games—in the 1926 fall classic and again in 1928. Both times it occurred in the fourth game and against the same team. What club were the Yankees playing?

Q155 What is Ruth's American League record for single-season shutouts by a southpaw?

Q156 On June 23, 1917, Ruth started, but never finished, pitching a game for the Boston Red Sox against the Washington Senators. For what is this game renowned?

Q157 Babe Ruth grew up at St. Mary's Industrial School for Boys in Baltimore. What famous entertainer also lived at the orphanage?

Q158 What were Babe Ruth's best numbers for stolen bases in one season?

Q159 In his first professional game, Ruth played for Baltimore in an exhibition game against the Brooklyn Dodgers. In his first at-bat, the Babe hit a fly ball to right field. Who caught the ball?

Q160 What Yankee surrendered the first home run pitch to the Red Sox's Babe Ruth in 1915?

Q161 Before Ruth set the single-season home run standard with 29 in 1919 (while with the Red Sox), who held the major league record?

Q162 The Yanks became the first club in major league history to hit over 100 home runs (115) in 1920. A large part of that success was due to new Yankee Babe Ruth and his 54 home runs. Whose record for homers did he eclipse that year?

Q163 Who was Babe Ruth's predecessor in the Yankee right field?

Q164 Who was on the mound when the Babe belted his first Yankee home run?

NEW YORK YANKEES

A153 .847 (388 total bases in 458 times at bat)

A154 St. Louis Cardinals

A155 Nine (1916)

A156 It is the only time two pitchers combined for a perfect game (After walking the first batter, Ruth was ejected for disputing the ump's abilities. Ernie Shore came in and, after picking off the base runner when he was attempting to steal, faced 26 consecutive batters without giving up a hit.)

A157 Al Jolson

A158 17 steals (twice in his career)

A159 Right fielder Casey Stengel

A160 Jack Warhop

A161 Philadelphia Phillie Gavvy Cravath (1915: 24 homers)

A162 His own (his last season with Boston, 1919, Ruth hit a record-high 29 homers)

A163 Harold "Nemo" Leibold

A164 Bosox pitcher and former teammate Herb Pennock (it was Babe's 50th career homer)

Q165   In 1920, Babe Ruth hit 54 home runs, and he followed with a 59-home-run season in 1921. During the 1920 season, he established a record for the greatest discrepency between the home run leader and the runner-up. In 1921, he matched that mark. What is the difference?

Q166   Which major league record did Babe Ruth NOT establish in 1921?

(a) Total bases on hits   (c) Runs scored
(b) Multiple-base hits   (d) Home runs

Q167   Babe Ruth was named team captain for six games in 1922. Who replaced him in that position for the rest of the season?

Q168   In honor of the grand opening of "The House That Ruth Built," the Babe hit a three-run homer to lead the Yanks over Boston before a crowd of 74,200 (April 18, 1923). What Sox pitcher gave up that hit?

Q169   How many times did Babe Ruth lead the league in batting average?

Q170   Who is the only pitcher to give up home runs to Babe Ruth in 1927 (the year he hit 60) while playing for two different clubs?

Q171   Name the pro football Hall of Famer who threw two home run pitches to Ruth in 1927.

Q172   Did Babe Ruth win the American League MVP award in 1927 (the year he hit 60 home runs)?

Q173   Babe Ruth hit his 60th homer of the season on September 30, 1927. That day also marked the last appearance of a Hall of Famer on the opposing team. Who was he?

Q174   Ruth's 60th homer came off a pitcher who would play for the Yankees the following season. Name him.

Q175   Babe Ruth hit his 500th home run in Cleveland on August 11, 1929. What other legend hit his 500th HR in the same city?

Q176   In a 14-year span (1918–31), Ruth won 13 slugging championships. Who was the only person to interrupt his string?

NEW YORK YANKEES

A165 There was a difference of 35 home runs between Ruth's league-leading total and the next highest batter's total.

A166 (c) The 177 runs scored is, however, an American League record. The major league records are (a) 457; (b) 119; (d) 59.

A167 Shortstop Everett Scott (Scott retained the title until 1925)

A168 Howard Ehmke

A169 Once (1924; he averaged .378)

A170 Tom Zachary (he yielded number 22 while with the St. Louis Browns, and later threw number 60 when he pitched for the Washington Senators)

A171 Ernie Nevers (while pitching for the St. Louis Browns, Nevers served up Ruth's eighth and 41st homers of the year)

A172 No (until 1929, no player could win the award twice. Since Ruth had won in 1923, he was ineligible, and the award was given to Gehrig)

A173 Walter Johnson (the Senator pitching great came in as a pinch-hitter in the ninth inning)

A174 Tom Zachary (1928–30)

A175 Ted Williams (June 17, 1960)

A176 St. Louis's Kenneth Williams (1925: .613)

Q177 The single most famous Ruth incident occurred during the 1932 World Series against the Chicago Cubs. On October 1, with Cub fans ridiculing him, Ruth pointed to a spot in the right-field bleachers and hit a home run there. Who were the Chicago pitcher and catcher on that memorable day?

Q178 What Red Sox pitcher did Babe Ruth defeat in his last major league pitching appearance (October 1, 1933)?

Q179 What Washington Senator pitched the last home run to Ruth while he was a Yankee (September 29, 1934)?

Q180 In Babe Ruth's final year of his professional career, he played for the 1935 Boston Braves. How many of his 714 home runs did he hit that year?

Q181 The last three home runs of Babe's career came in a single game. Name the Pittsburgh pitchers who gave up the homers to the then Boston Brave.

Q182 The Babe's playing career ended on May 30, 1935, in the first game of a doubleheader between the Braves and the Phillies. Who was the last man to throw a regular-season pitch to Ruth?

Q183 The final team Ruth played for was the Boston Braves, but it was not the last organization to sign him as a coach and a player. Who used the Bambino as a gate attraction?

Q184 Who served up the last pitch to Babe Ruth?

Q185 How many times did Ruth establish a major league record for home runs in a season?

Q186 While with Boston, Ruth became the only pitcher to lead the majors in home runs in one season. How many did he belt to lead the way in 1918?

—THE IRON MAN—

Q187 In how many seasons did Lou Gehrig belt 200 hits or more?

Q188 Who is the only pitcher to surrender two of Lou Gehrig's major-league-record career 23 grand slams?

NEW YORK YANKEES

A177 Pitcher: Charlie Root; catcher: Gabby Hartnett (the next batter was Lou Gehrig, and he promptly belted a homer as well)

A178 Bob Kline

A179 Syd Cohen (the homer, his 708th, was his last in the American League)

A180 Six

A181 Red Lucas (1) and Guy Bush (2) (May 25, 1935; five days later, Ruth retired as a player from the game)

A182 Jim Bivin (Ruth grounded out to first baseman Dolph Camilli and left the game soon afterward)

A183 Brooklyn Dodgers (Ruth took batting practice, played in exhibition games, and coached first base, but never played in a regular-season game with the team)

A184 Boston Brave Johnny Sain (July 28, 1943; in an exhibition game at Yankee Stadium, the Bambino got a base on balls after a foul strike)

A185 Four times (1919, when he surpassed Philadelphia's Socks Seybold's total of 16; 1920 and 1921, when he hit 54 and 59 homers respectively; and 1927, when he hit 60 homers)

A186 11 home runs

A187 Eight (1927, 1928, 1930, 1931, 1932, 1934, 1936, and 1937)

A188 Lloyd Brown (while pitching for the Senators and Indians)

Q189 What Yankee held the record for the consecutive-game streak prior to Gehrig?

Q190 Lou Gehrig's first appearance in pinstripes occurred on May 30, 1925, when he came into the game as a pinch-hitter. For whom was he batting?

Q191 On June 1, 1925, Lou Gehrig began his "Iron Man" legend of playing in 2,130 consecutive games. Whom did he replace on the field?

Q192 Who replaced Gehrig at first base on May 2, 1939?

Q193 Name the present-day player who has tied Lou Gehrig's American League record of four three-home-run games in a career.

—JOLTIN' JOE—

Q194 Whose major league record did DiMaggio surpass when he set his 56-game hitting streak?

Q195 How many bases did DiMaggio steal in his 13-year career?

Q196 How many league MVP awards did DiMaggio win during his 13 years with the Yankees?

Q197 The "Yankee Clipper's" record of hitting safely in 56 consecutive games is a major league mark. DiMaggio also set a consecutive game hitting record while playing for the San Francisco Seals of the Pacific Coast League in 1933. What was that record?

Q198 How did "Joltin' Joe" come to play with the Yankees?

Q199 What number did DiMaggio first wear before he switched to No. 5?

Q200 Whom did Joe D. get his first hit off to begin the 56-game streak?

Q201 Name the two Cleveland pitchers who combined to stop DiMaggio's streak on July 17, 1941.

NEW YORK YANKEES

A189 Shortstop Everett Scott (his record was 1,307 games)

A190 Pee Wee Wanninger

A191 Wally Pipp

A192 Babe Dahlgren

A193 Joe Carter

A194 Wee Willie Keeler (44 games)

A195 30 times

A196 Three (1939, 1941, 1947)

A197 61 consecutive games with a hit

A198 The team acquired him from San Francisco of the Pacific Coast League for $25,000 and five cast-off players in November 1934. He debuted with New York in 1936.

A199 No. 9

A200 White Sox pitcher Edgar Smith (a first-inning single)

A201 Al Smith (starter who held DiMaggio hitless in two official at-bats and walked him) and Jim Bagby, Jr. (who, in the eighth inning, induced DiMaggio to hit into a double play)

—THE MICK—

Q202 Mickey Mantle was known for his hitting prowess from both sides of the plate. How many times did he hit a home run from both the left and right side of the plate in the same game?

Q203 Mickey Mantle set a record for hitting safely in consecutive All-Star Games. What standard did the Mick establish?

Q204 In his 18-year career, how many times did Mickey Mantle lead the American League in home runs?

Q205 Mantle is listed as having hit the longest recorded home run in baseball—565 feet from the plate. Against what team and pitcher did he register this feat?

Q206 How many seasons did Mantle play first base?

Q207 Mickey Mantle is one of two switch-hitters to win the American League MVP. Who is the other? (Hint: He is not a Yankee and is not known for his hitting.)

Q208 The Mick's first season with the Yankees was 1951. Whom did he join in the outfield?

Q209 On April 4, 1965, Mickey recorded another of his league firsts while playing against the Houston Astros. What did he do?

Q210 What did Mantle keep in his back pocket when he played a game?

GLORY DAYS

Q211 How many times have the Yankees played in the World Series?

Q212 How many times have the Yankees been world champions?

Q213 How many times have the Yankees swept the Series in four straight?

NEW YORK YANKEES

---------------------- · ----------------------

A202 10 times

A203 Seven (Joe Morgan later tied the record)

A204 Four (1955, 1956, 1958, and 1960)

A205 Washington Senators; Chuck Stobbs (at Griffith Stadium)

A206 Two (he switched to first in 1967 and played his last season at the infield position)

A207 Oakland's Vida Blue

A208 Jackie Jensen (LF) and Joe DiMaggio (CF)

A209 He hit the first home run in a domed stadium

A210 A rabbit's foot

---------------------- · ----------------------

A211 33 times

A212 22 times

A213 Six (1927, 1928, 1932, 1938, 1939, and 1950)

Q214 The Yankees have played in 187 World Series games (won: 109, lost: 77, tied: 1). What team is second?

Q215 Whom have the Yankees met and defeated the most times in World Series play?

Q216 Two teams have defeated the Yankees three times in World Series competition. Who are they?

Q217 How many times have the Yankees lost the World Series four games to none?

Q218 Name the only team to defeat the Yankees in back-to-back World Series.

Q219 Name the only starting pitcher in a World Series game who did not bat ninth in the order.

Q220 The 1927 Series between the Yankees and Pirates is the only fall classic to end on a wild pitch. Name the Pittsburgh pitcher and the player who scored from third.

Q221 Two Yankees are among three pitchers who have won final World Series games in consecutive years. Name them.

Q222 Name the Yankee who was the first pinch-hitter to bang out a home run in the World Series.

Q223 The Yankee domination of the 1927 season extended into the World Series, as New York swept four straight games from their National League opponents. Whom did they beat that year?

Q224 This Yankee stole home twice in a World Series—once in 1921 and again in 1928. Who achieved this unequaled feat?

Q225 In Game 6 of the 1947 Series, Dodger Al Gionfriddo made a sensational catch on Joe DiMaggio in the sixth inning to stop the Yankees' comeback and win the game 8–6. What two Yanks were on base when the play occurred?

Q226 In the 1953 Series against Brooklyn, Billy Martin's hit in the ninth won the game and the championship for the Yankees. Who scored to give the Yanks the 4–3 victory?

NEW YORK YANKEES

A214 Giants (N.Y. and S.F.)—93 games (in the American League, the Boston Red Sox are second with 60 games)

A215 Dodgers (the Yankees have won eight of the 11 matches)

A216 Dodgers (1955, 1963, 1981) and Cardinals (1926, 1942, 1964)

A217 Three times (1922: N.Y. Giants; 1963: L.A. Dodgers; 1976: Cincinnati Reds)

A218 New York Giants (1921 and 1922; the Yanks gained revenge by defeating their crosstown rivals in 1923 for their first major league crown)

A219 Babe Ruth (in his last Series appearance as a pitcher in 1918, he batted sixth for the Red Sox against the Cubs)

A220 John Miljus threw a wild pitch to allow Earle Combs to score (At the time, Tony Lazzeri was at the plate. The Yanks swept the Series by winning the game, 4–3.)

A221 Lefty Gomez (1936 and 1937) and Allie Reynolds (1952 and 1953) (The other pitcher who achieved this distinction is New York Giant Art Nehf in the 1921 and 1922 Series against the Yankees)

A222 Yogi Berra (October 2, 1947: agaianst Brooklyn)

A223 Pittsburgh Pirates

A224 Bob Meusel

A225 Yogi Berra and George Stirnweiss (the Yankees won the championship in the seventh game)

A226 Hank Bauer

Q227 During the 1956 Series, the Yankees used eight different pitchers. How many of the New York hurlers gave complete-game performances?

Q228 Don Larsen threw the only perfect game in World Series history on October 8, 1956, against the Brooklyn Dodgers. Who was the batter on the final out?

Q229 Who was the catcher in Don Larsen's 1956 World Series perfect game?

Q230 Name the umpire who was behind the plate for Larsen's perfect game in the 1956 Series.

Q231 The seventh game of the 1960 Series was determined by a home run in the bottom of the ninth. Who homered over the Forbes Field left-field wall to ensure victory for the Pirates?

Q232 What unequaled feat did the Boyer brothers achieve in the 1964 World Series? (Clete played for New York, while Ken was a Cardinal.)

Q233 In Game 4 of the 1964 World Series, with New York leading 3–0, the hidden ball trick was employed to pick off a Yankee at second base. Name the Yankee who was put out and the St. Louis Cardinal who caught him napping.

Q234 In the game cited above, a Cardinal grand slam was the decisive hit in St. Louis's win that day. Who was the New York pitcher, and which Cardinal hit the base-clearer?

Q235 Whom did the Yankees defeat in the American League Championship Series in three consecutive years—1976, 1977, and 1978?

Q236 A bottom-of-the-ninth home run determined the 1976 American League pennant winner. What Yankee hit the homer, who was the opposing team, and what was unique about the winning run?

Q237 Who gave up the game-winning homer in the previous question?

Q238 In Game 1 of the 1976 Series, the Yankees used the first designated hitter in World Series history. Name the batter.

Q239 Who is the only player to hit a home run in his only at-bat in the World Series?

NEW YORK YANKEES

A227 Five—Game 3: Whitey Ford; Game 4: Tom Sturdivant; Game 5: Don Larsen; Game 6: Bob Turley (lost); Game 7: Johnny Kucks

A228 Pinch-hitter Dale Mitchell (batting for Sal Maglie, he took a called strike three)

A229 Yogi Berra

A230 Babe Pinelli (he retired after the 1956 season)

A231 Bill Mazeroski (off Ralph Terry—this is the only time the World Series has ended on a home run)

A232 They are the only brothers to hit home runs in the same Series (and they did it in the same game—Game 7!)

A233 Shortstop Dick Groat caught Mickey Mantle with the ploy (the play is credited with turning the Series' momentum in St. Louis's favor as the Cardinals went on to win the game and the Series)

A234 Ken Boyer hit the grand slam home run off Al Downing in the sixth for a 4–3 win

A235 Kansas City Royals

A236 Chris Chambliss belted the hit against the Kansas City Royals. Chambliss never touched third base or home plate because both were dug up as souvenirs by the fans as they poured onto the field.

A237 Mark Littell

A238 Lou Piniella (he had a double to lead off the second inning)

A239 Jim Mason (Game 3 of the 1976 Series; Mason homered off Reds pitcher Pat Zachry in the seventh inning)

Q240 Thurman Munson set the major league postseason record in 1976 with 19 hits. Who broke his mark in the 1986 playoffs?

Q241 The first game of the 1977 Series ended in the bottom of the 12th inning with the Yanks on top, 4–3. Who hit the game-winning RBI?

Q242 Mr. October hit three home runs in the sixth game of the 1977 Series. What did all three of Jackson's dingers have in common?

Q243 Reggie Jackson hit three home runs in Game 6 of the 1977 Series and equaled Babe Ruth's feat (Ruth did it twice—1926 and 1928). Name the three Dodgers who served up the pitches.

Q244 True or false. The 1978 Yankees were the first team in World Series history to win four straight games after losing the opening two matches.

Q245 It was a single game that determined the 1978 Eastern Division champion as the Yankees, led by Bucky Dent's three-run homer, defeated Boston in a one-game playoff. Name the pitcher who gave up Dent's home run.

Q246 When Bucky Dent hit his famous home run in the seventh inning, who was on base?

Q247 On October 2, 1978, the Yankees played Boston in a one game playoff to determine the AL East Division Champion. Who were the starting pitchers on both teams?

Q248 Name the Yankee who hit the game-winning home run and the losing hurler who served up the pitch in the 1978 playoff game against the Boston Red Sox.

Q249 What pitcher was credited with the win in New York's 5–4 victory?

Q250 Who replaced the injured Willie Randolph at second base in the 1978 Series?

Q251 Due to the players' strike, a preliminary playoff round was added to the 1981 schedule. Whom did New York defeat in that best-of-five series?

Q252 The aging Yankees went down in six games in the team's losing 1981 Series. What starter epitomized New York's futility by going 1-for-25?

NEW YORK YANKEES

A240 Boston's Marty Barrett

A241 Paul Blair (his single drove in Willie Randolph)

A242 Each was hit on the first pitch thrown to Jackson

A243 Burt Hooten (two-run homer in the fourth), Elias Sosa (two-run homer in the fifth), and Charlie Hough (in the eighth)

A244 True (the Dodgers would match this feat in the 1981 Series against the Yankees)

A245 Mike Torrez (Dent hit a two-out three-run homer in the seventh inning with the count at 0–2)

A246 Roy White and Chris Chambliss

A247 Ron Guidry and Mike Torrez

A248 Reggie Jackson's home run to the centerfield bleachers came off Bob Stanley

A249 Rick Gossage

A250 Brian Doyle (Doyle, who had a .192 average in 52 regular season at-bats, finished the Series with an incredible .438 average)

A251 Milwaukee Brewers (Yankees won, 3–2.)

A252 Dave Winfield

Q253   The Yankees jumped to a 3–0 lead in the first inning of the opening game of the 1981 World Series. Who slammed the three-run dinger?

Q254   After New York's sweep of Oakland in the 1981 AL Championship Series, the team held a postgame celebration. What two players came to blows at the party?

Q255   Who were the only two Yankees to play in all four World Series between 1976 and 1981?

Q256   The American League record for single-season victories by a pitcher is 41. Name the Yankee who set the record in 1904.

Q257   In 1927, the Yankees established an AL record with 110 victories. Who would surpass that mark by one game in 1954?

Q258   Name the Hall of Fame outfielder whose single-season team record of 231 hits was broken by Don Mattingly in 1986.

Q259   The American League title for RBIs in a single season is 184. Who established this mark?

Q260   In what year did the Yankees set the major league record for runs scored in a single season?

Q261   This Yankee holds the highest major league single season batting average at his position—catcher. Name him.

Q262   What is the greatest number of players from one club placed on the All-Star team in any one year?

Q263   The Yankees hold the standard for most homers in a 162-game season. What is the record?

Q264   Whitey Ford still holds the major league record for fewest losses at the 100-win mark. How many did he have?

Q265   Name the pitcher who set the record for consecutive relief appearances without a start.

Q266   What Yankee pitcher once held the American League record (since broken) of 272 consecutive starts without a relief appearance?

NEW YORK YANKEES

A253   Bob Watson (off Jerry Reuss)

A254   Graig Nettles and Reggie Jackson (Nettles resented how Jackson's friends were treating his family and popped Mr. October)

A255   Lou Pinella and Graig Nettles

A256   Jack Chesbro (he lost 12 games that year)

A257   Cleveland Indians

A258   Earle Combs (his 1927 record stood until Mattingly hit 238)

A259   Lou Gehrig (1931)

A260   1931 (they scored 1,067 runs—an average of 6.9 runs per game)

A261   Bill Dickey (1936: .362)

A262   Nine Yankees (twice: 1939 and 1942)

A263   240 home runs (1961)

A264   36 losses

A265   Sparky Lyle (From 1967 through 1982, he was sent in for relief in 899 consecutive appearences. In his entire career, he never started a game.)

A266   Mel Stottlemyre

Q267 What two center fielders share the team record for fewest double-play grounders in one season?

Q268 Whose major league record did Don Mattingly tie when he hit home runs in eight consecutive games during the 1987 season?

Q269 Which player holds the major league record for most consecutive errorless games by a catcher?

Q270 Who surpassed Lou Gehrig's major league record of three consecutive seasons with 200 hits and 100 bases-on-balls?

Q271 Don Mattingly set a major league mark when he blasted six grand slams during the 1989 season. Whose record did he shatter?

Q272 Yogi Berra's American League career mark of 306 homers by a catcher was surpassed on June 21, 1989, at Yankee Stadium. Who broke Berra's record?

Q273 This slugger has the distinction of striking out more often than anyone in major league history. Who is he and from whom did he wrest the title?

Q274 Ruth or Gehrig? Match the correct player with the batting category in which he leads the Yankees.

(a) Runs (1,959) (e) Total Bases (5,131)
(b) Hits (2,721) (f) RBIs (1,991)
(c) Doubles (535) (g) Extra Base Hits (1,190)
(d) Triples (162) (h) Career Batting Average (.349)

NEW YORK YANKEES

A267 Mickey Mantle (1961) and Mickey Rivers (1977)

A268 Dale Long (of Pittsburgh)

A269 Rick Cerone: 159 games (from July 5, 1987, while with the Yankees, to May 8, 1989, while playing for Boston)

A270 Boston's Wade Boggs (1986–89)

A271 Cub Ernie Banks (1955) and Oriole Jim Gentile (1961)

A272 Carlton Fisk

A273 Reggie Jackson; the former leader was Willie Stargell

A274 Ruth: (a), (e), (h).
Gehrig: (b), (c), (d), (f), (g).

Brooklyn Dodgers

DODGERS

Q1 What owner moved the team from Brooklyn to the West Coast?

Q2 What Dodger manager appeared in a record nine All-Star Games as the National League pilot?

Q3 In 1947, manager Leo Durocher was suspended for the season because he was linked to gambling activities. Name the commissioner who punished Leo the Lip.

Q4 Name the two men who replaced Durocher as Dodger manager for the 1947 season.

Q5 Dodger manager Walter Alston made only one appearance as a player in a major league game. For what team did he play?

Q6 Who was the Dodgers' last manager in Brooklyn (1957)?

Q7 In Alston's only pro appearance, he replaced a player who was ejected from the game in the seventh inning. Name the first baseman who was thrown out.

Q8 When Ebbets Field was opened in 1913, it soon became apparent that the architect omitted one detail. What was left out of the design and construction?

Q9 In 1915, the Dodgers picked up a nickname based on its manager. What was the team called?

BROOKLYN DODGERS

A1   Owner Walter O'Malley

A2   Walter Alston

A3   A. B. "Happy" Chandler

A4   Clyde Sukeforth (for three games) and Burt Shotton

A5   St. Louis Cardinals

A6   Walter Alston (he managed from 1954 to 1957 on the East Coast before guiding the Dodgers through the 1976 season in L.A.)

A7   Johnny Mize (in his sole at-bat, Alston struck out against the Chicago Cubs' Lon Warneke)

A8   A press box

A9   The Robins (after manager Wilbert Robinson)

Q10 In 1934, the Dodgers knocked the Giants out of the pennant race. Besides the ever-present rivalry between the two teams, the victory had special significance because of a statement made by Giant manager Bill Terry. What infuriated the Dodgers?

Q11 In the first game of a 1938 doubleheader against the Cardinals, the Dodgers tested a new ball. What was different about it?

Q12 The first Dodger night game was on June 15, 1938. For what other distinction is the game noted in baseball history?

Q13 In that game, who made the last Dodger out?

Q14 Whom did the Dodgers meet in the first ever televised game on August 26, 1939?

Q15 Who announced the first radio broadcast of a Dodger regular-season game (April 18, 1939)?

Q16 During the 1957 season, owner Walter O'Malley moved seven Dodger home games away from Ebbets Field to protest the conditions there. Where did the team play those contests?

Q17 Who announced they would move first from New York to the West Coast, the Giants or the Dodgers?

Q18 On September 29, 1957, the Brooklyn Dodgers played their last game. Name the starting pitcher, his reliever, and the Dodger who scored the team's last run.

Q19 The longest game in major league history was played between the Dodgers and the Braves at Boston on May 1, 1920. Darkness halted the game after 26 innings with the score knotted at 1–1. Name the pitchers who went the distance for both teams.

Q20 How did Hall of Famer Arthur Vance acquire the nickname "Dazzy"?

Q21 Giant Carl Hubbell won 24 consecutive games (a major league record) before a Dodger pitcher defeated him on May 31, 1937. Who stopped the streak?

Q22 In his last major league game, he threw a one-hitter while facing 27 batters (the only runner was doubled up) in a 6–0 win. Who was this hurler?

BROOKLYN DODGERS

A10 Terry asked whether Brooklyn was still in the league; the comment became a Dodger rallying cry for team and fans alike

A11 It was yellow instead of white (the Dodgers won the game 6–2, but the colorful ball was never used again)

A12 It was the second consecutive no-hitter thrown by Cincinnati's Johnny Vander Meer (he no-hit the Boston Bees, 3–0, on June 11, and followed it with a 5–0 no-hitter against Brooklyn)

A13 Leo Durocher

A14 Cincinnati Reds (The Reds won 5–2, with pitcher Luke Hamlin taking the loss. Station W2XBS aired only three commercials: for Ivory Soap, Mobil Oil, and Wheaties.)

A15 Red Barber (the Dodgers lost to the Giants, 7–3)

A16 Roosevelt Stadium in Jersey City

A17 The Giants (Horace Stoneham, president of the Giants, made his announcement on August 20, 1957, while Dodger president Walter O'Malley made his announcement on October 8 of the same year)

A18 Starter: Roger Craig; reliever: Sandy Koufax; final run: Jim Gilliam (the Dodgers lost at Philadelphia, 2–1)

A19 Dodgers: Leon Cadore; Braves: Joe Oeschger

A20 He picked it up from his blazing fastball called "the dazzler"

A21 Fred Frankhouse

A22 Larry French (shortly after pitching the game on September 23, 1942, French entered the Navy and never returned to pro baseball)

Q23 Who was the first pitcher honored with the Cy Young Award?

Q24 What Dodger was the National League ERA leader in 1957?

Q25 What Dodger gave up more home runs to Hank Aaron (17) than any other pitcher?

Q26 What current manager was the last pitcher of record for the Brooklyn Dodgers?

Q27 Ebbets Field was opened on April 5, 1913, in an exhibition game against the Yankees. Who hit the first home run in the park?

Q28 After being traded to Pittsburgh, Casey Stengel made his initial return to Ebbets Field a memorable one. In his first at-bat, he stepped out of the box and called time out. What did he do next?

Q29 This Dodger is one of two players to hit for the cycle three times. Who was he?

Q30 Who was the first Dodger named to the All-Star Game in 1933?

Q31 This Dodger was not only the first to start in an All-Star game, in 1938, but is the only player to hit a bunt home run in the annual event. Name him.

Q32 Jackie Robinson was the first black to play in the major leagues, but before he was moved up to Brooklyn he spent one year in the International League (where he was also the first black). With what team did Robinson develop his skills?

Q33 Jackie Robinson played in his first major league game on April 11, 1947. Whom did the Dodgers meet in the exhibition contest?

Q34 The 1949 All-Star Game, played at Ebbets Field, featured the first blacks to appear in the annual match-up. Three represented the Dodgers. Who were the trendsetting players?

Q35 In 1950, and again in 1953, three Dodgers hit more than 30 home runs in one season. Name the trio. (Hint: They are the same for both years.)

BROOKLYN DODGERS

A23   Don Newcombe (1956: 27–7, 3.06 ERA)

A24   Johnny Podres

A25   Don Drysdale

A26   Roger Craig (he lost to the Phillies, 2–1, on September 29, 1957, at Philadelphia)

A27   Casey Stengel (it was an inside-the-park homer)

A28   He lifted his cap and a bird flew out

A29   Babe Herman (He achieved it twice in 1931 and once in 1933. He is tied with the Yankees' Bob Meusel.)

A30   Tony Cuccinello (he struck out pinch-hitting for Carl Hubbell in the ninth)

A31   Leo Durocher (he was also the first Dodger skipper to manage in an All-Star Game)

A32   Montreal Royals

A33   The Yankess

A34   Jackie Robinson, Roy Campanella, and Don Newcombe (they were joined on the field by Cleveland's Larry Doby)

A35   1950: Gil Hodges (32), Duke Snider (31), Roy Campanella (31); 1953: Snider (42), Campanella (41), Hodges (31)

Q36 What Dodger never played in a major league game but was ejected from one?

Q37 What first baseman played only one game for the Dodgers in 1949 and later went on to fame and fortune in television?

Q38 Pee Wee Reese appeared in eight All-Star matches during his career. How many hits did he get in those games?

Q39 The last player to hit a home run in Ebbets Field was a Dodger on September 22, 1957. Name the batter.

Q40 How many times did Jackie Robinson steal home in his career?

Q41 Who was the last Brooklyn Dodger to retire from the L.A. team?

Q42 The only triple play in Series history took place in 1920. What Dodger pitcher hit into the inning killer?

Q43 What Dodger pitcher gave up the first grand slam homer in World Series play in Game 5 of the 1920 classic?

Q44 Dodger catcher Mickey Owen hit the first pinch-hit homer in All-Star history (1942). What is surprising about his achievement?

Q45 What team squeaked by the Dodgers in a three-game playoff for the right to meet the Boston Red Sox in the 1946 World Series?

Q46 Yankee Bill Bevens almost became the first pitcher to hurl a World Series no-hitter in the 1947 Series. Name the Brooklyn Dodger who broke up Bevens's attempt and won the game with one hit.

Q47 The 1951 season ended with a bang and a three-game playoff loss to the Giants. With the Dodgers ahead 4–2, one out, and two men on base, Bobby Thomson hit "the shot heard 'round the world." Who gave up the heroic home run hit?

Q48 Who was the first black pitcher to win a World Series game?

Q49 In the 1953 Series, the Dodgers lost the sixth game and the Series when Billy Martin got a one-out hit in the ninth. Who was the losing pticher in the 4–3 game?

BROOKLYN DODGERS

A36 Bill Sharman (A reserve who never got in a game, Sharman was ejected in 1951 during a bench-clearing brawl. After the season, he decided to concentrate on another sport and went on to become a Hall of Famer with the Boston Celtics.)

A37 Chuck Connors (better known as "the Rifleman"; Connors also played 66 games with the Chicago Cubs in 1951)

A38 Two (both hits came in his last appearance, in 1953)

A39 Duke Snider (he hit two homers that day)

A40 19 times

A41 Pitcher Don Drysdale (August 11, 1969)

A42 Clarence Mitchell (in the fifth game of the Series, Mitchell accounted for eight outs after he hit into a double play later in the contest)

A43 Burleigh Grimes (to Cleveland's Elmer Smith)

A44 Owen did not hit a home run in 133 regular-season games that year

A45 St. Louis Cardinals (the Cardinals swept two straight games)

A46 Cookie Lavagetto (Cookie hit a two-RBI double with two out in the bottom of the ninth)

A47 Ralph Branca

A48 Dodger Joe Black (in Game 1 of the 1952 Series against the Yankees, he threw a six-hitter and won, 4–2)

A49 Clem Labine

Q50 The Dodgers' only world title came in a Subway Series against the Yankees in 1955. In the seventh game, a reserve left fielder killed a Yankee rally with the Dodgers ahead 2–0 by making a sensational catch and then doubling up a base runner. Who was this fielder?

Q51 Don Zimmer was removed from the seventh game of the '55 Series in favor of a pinch-hitter. Who came in to bat for him?

Q52 Who is the only man to play in all 44 games of the seven World Series (from 1941 through 1956) between the Brooklyn Dodgers and the Yankees?

Q53 The Dodgers were on the losing end of Don Larsen's perfect game in the 1956 World Series. Who were the last three Brooklyn batters in that game?

Q54 Only two players, one from each team, participated in both the 1951 and the 1962 National League playoffs between the Giants and the Dodgers. Who were they?

Q55 The Dodger who won the 1944 batting championship had a brother who took the batting crown three years later. It is the only time that siblings have done this. Name the Dodger half of the duo.

Q56 Name the Dodger who shares the season record for stealing home plate with Minnesota's Rod Carew.

Q57 Dan Bankhead started his career with the Dodgers on August 26, 1947. What place does he hold in major league history?

Q58 In 1952, the Dodgers set a major league record for runs by one team in the first inning. How many did they score against the Reds?

Q59 What Dodger was the last pitcher to steal home in the majors?

Q60 Willie Mays hit home run No. 512 at Candlestick Park on May 4, 1966, to break Mel Ott's National League record. What Dodger pitcher gave up the celebrated homer?

Q61 Name the former Dodger and one-time manager who holds the season record for sacrifice flies.

Q62 What Dodger struck out the most consecutive times at bat?

BROOKLYN DODGERS

A50   Sandy Amoros (after catching the fly ball in the deep left-field corner, Amoros turned and fired the relay to shortstop Pee Wee Reese, whose throw to Gil Hodges at first caught the runner cold)

A51   George Shuba

A52   Shortstop Pee Wee Reese

A53   Carl Furillo, Roy Campanella, and Dale Mitchell

A54   Giant Willie Mays and Dodger Duke Snider

A55   Dixie Walker (his brother, Harry, who played most of the year with the Phillies after starting the season with the Cardinals, won the honor in 1947)

A56   Pete Reiser (in 1946, he stole home seven times)

A57   He was the first black pitcher in the major leagues

A58   15 runs (they went on to win, 19–1)

A59   Don Newcombe (May 26, 1955: at Pittsburgh; Brooklyn won, 6–2)

A60   Claude Osteen

A61   Gil Hodges (1954: 19)

A62   Sandy Koufax (1955: 12 straight times, a big-league standard)

Q63   Who is the only Dodger to hit three homers in a game twice?

Q64   What Dodger recorded the last no-hitter at Ebbets Field?

Q65   What distinction does L.A. Dodger Bill Russell share with Brooklyn Dodger Jackie Robinson?

Q66   In 1918, the Dodgers swapped future Hall of Fame players with the Pittsburgh Pirates. Name the two players involved in the transaction.

Q67   On October 5, 1937, the Dodgers sent Joe Stripp, Jimmy Bucher, Johnny Cooney, and pitcher Roy Henshaw to the St. Louis Cardinals for one player. Whom did Brooklyn receive in return?

Q68   On December 13, 1956, the Dodgers traded Jackie Robinson. To what team and for what player was Robinson swapped?

Q69   The Dodgers obtained former Giant Sal Maglie from the Cleveland Indians in May 1956. To what team did they sell the pitcher in 1957?

Q70   Duke Snider ended his Dodger career on April 1, 1963, when he was sold by the club for $40,000. What team purchased Snider?

BROOKLYN DODGERS

A63   Duke Snider

A64   Sal Maglie (1956: 5–0, against Philadelphia)

A65   They are the only Dodgers to strike out five times in a game

A66   Casey Stengel went to the Pirates for Burleigh Grimes

A67   Leo Durocher

A68   New York Giants; pitcher Dick Littlefield (Robinson retired less than a month later, which voided the transaction)

A69   The Yankees

A70   The Mets

New York Giants

Q27. It was the "shot heard 'round the world" as Bobby Thomson hit a three-run homer to give the Giants a 5–4 victory over the Dodgers and the 1951 pennant. It ranks as one of the greatest pennant-winning comebacks in baseball history. What two players were on base?

GIANTS

Q1 John McGraw was a staple with the Giants. How many seasons did he manage the team before he became gravely ill and was forced to retire?

Q2 Name the New York manager who was the first to be ejected from two games in one day.

Q3 Whom did Leo Durocher replace as manager of the Giants in the middle of the 1948 season?

Q4 Who was the last manager of the New York Giants?

Q5 In 1903, Joe "Iron Man" McGinnity earned his nickname when he set a modern NL record by pitching in 434 innings in one season. How many complete doubleheaders did McGinnity throw that year?

Q6 This Giant hurler was the first major league pitcher to be hired solely for relief duty. Name him.

Q7 How many consecutive victories did Giant Rube Marquard pitch over the Dodgers?

Q8 Name the Giant pitcher who was known as the "Meal Ticket."

Q9 Carl Hubbell played 18 years with the Giants and set a number of team and league records. He will always be remembered for striking out five of baseball's all-time greats in succession during the 1934 All-Star Game. Name the quintet who went down swinging.

NEW YORK GIANTS

A1   31 seasons (1902–32; in that time, he won 10 NL pennants)

A2   Mel Ott (June 9, 1946: a doubleheader against Pittsburgh)

A3   Mel Ott (Durocher left the Dodgers to become New York's manager when Ott was fired on July 16, 1948)

A4   Bill Rigney (he managed the club from 1956 until June 1960 with San Francisco)

A5   Three (and he won all six games!)

A6   Otis Crandall (1908–18)

A7   19 victories

A8   Carl Hubbell

A9   Babe Ruth, Lou Gehrig, Jimmie Foxx, Al Simmons, and Joe Cronin

Q10 This Giant pitcher is the only player to give up back-to-back homers to two brothers. Name him.

Q11 Hoyt Wilhelm hit a home run in his first major league at-bat (April 23, 1952) against Boston Brave pitcher Dick Hoover. How many more did Wilhelm connect on in his 21 seasons and 432 career at-bats?

Q12 What pitcher was known for his "flutter ball"?

Q13 As a rookie in 1952, this pitcher was the first reliever to win an ERA title. Who was he?

Q14 Philadelphia's Danny Litwhiler is the only player to hit a ball over the roof of the double-deck left-field bleachers at the Polo Grounds—more than 505 feet. Name the Giant pitcher who served up the homer.

Q15 What was Hall of Famer Frankie Frisch's nickname?

Q16 Name the Giant who was a star running back at LSU in the 1940s while pro football Hall of Famer Steve Van Buren was on the same team.

Q17 One of baseball's most famous scenes involves Willie Mays making an over-the-head grab of a deep fly ball and, in a single motion, turning to throw the ball to home plate. Who was the batter, and what runner was on third base attempting to go home?

Q18 Two 1954 Giants finished 1–2 for the National League batting title. Who were they?

Q19 Who got the final hit in the last match-up between the New York Giants and the Brooklyn Dodgers at the Polo Grounds on September 8, 1957?

Q20 How many Gold Glove Awards did Willie Mays win in his career?

Q21 What Giant pitcher threw three shutouts in six days to lead New York over the Philadelphia Athletics in the 1905 World Series?

Q22 In 1908, "Merkle's Boner" cost the Giants the National League pennant. What was Merkle's Boner?

NEW YORK GIANTS

A10 Cliff Melton (September 15, 1938: he threw home run pitchers to brothers Lloyd and Paul Waner of the Pirates)

A11 None

A12 Hoyt Wilhelm (he was a Giant from 1952 to 1957)

A13 Hoyt Wilhelm (2.36 ERA)

A14 Ace Adams

A15 The Fordham Flash (because he attended Fordham University)

A16 Alvin Dark

A17 Dodger Carl Furillo hit the 330-foot drive, and Billy Cox was on third (Cox, never expecting the ball to be caught, was most of the way home. Though he wasn't thrown out, he returned to third and never scored in the game. Catcher Wes Westrum fielded the throw on one hop.)

A18 Willie Mays (.345) and Don Mueller (.342)

A19 Willie Mays (he hit a triple)

A20 12 awards

A21 Christy Mathewson

A22 Fred Merkle, who was on first, began to celebrate and never touched second base. Cub second baseman Johnny Evers grabbed the ball and touched second, and had Merkle called out. The game ended in a tie and had to be replayed later because the fans took over the field. The Giants lost the last five games of the season, as well as the makeup game with Chicago, costing the team the pennant.

Q23 The 1924 World Series between New York and Washington was lost in the seventh game because this Giant catcher stepped on his discarded mask and dropped a foul ball behind the plate. Name the player who was blamed for the loss.

Q24 One of the most remarkable catches captured on film is that of Mays making an over-the-shoulder grab in the opening game of the 1954 World Series. It occurred in the eighth inning, with the score tied 2–2. Name the Cleveland Indian who hit the fly ball.

Q25 Who was the only man to play in the last World Series game for both the New York Giants (1954) and the Brooklyn Dodgers (1956)?

Q26 What pinch-hitter went four for six in three games and had seven RBIs in the 1954 Series against the Indians?

Q27 It was the "shot heard 'round the world" as Bobby Thomson hit a three-run homer to give the Giants a 5–4 victory over the Dodgers and the 1951 pennant. It ranks as one of the greatest pennant-winning comebacks in baseball history. What two players were on base?

Q28 The 1893 Giants were by far the most prolific base-stealing team in the history of the sport. What is their record?

Q29 The NL record for hits in a game by a team that was shut out was set by the Giants in a game against Chicago. How many scoreless hits did they get?

Q30 Name the Giant who was the first 20-year-old to have a 20-win season.

Q31 The only morning no-hitter was registered by this Giant in 1908 against Philadelphia. Name the early-bird hurler.

Q32 What was Christy Mathewson's pitching record for consecutive innings without giving up a walk?

Q33 From September 7 until September 30, 1916, the Giants set a major league record by winning 26 consecutive games. Who were the first and last winning pitchers in the streak?

Q34 The Giants established a major league record for the shortest nine-inning victory. Whom did they defeat, and how long did it take?

NEW YORK GIANTS

A23   Hank Gowdy (After Gowdy tripped over his mask, Muddy Ruel doubled to left on the succeeding pitch. The next batter, Earl McNeely, hit a pitch off Giant Jack Bentley to score Ruel and win the Series.)

A24   First baseman Vic Wertz (After Mays's catch, Larry Doby tagged up from second and went to third, but never scored. The Giants beat the Indians 5–2 in 10 innings and swept the Series.)

A25   Dale Mitchell (In 1954, he was a pinch-hitter for Cleveland, and, in 1956, he pinch-hit for Brooklyn. He was on the losing side in both cases.)

A26   Dusty Rhodes (in each game he batted for left fielder Monte Irvin)

A27   Alvin Dark, who singled to open the bottom of the ninth, and Clint Hartung, a reserve who was running for the injured Don Mueller

A28   426 bases (In comparison, the American League record is held by the Oakland A's with 341 bases stolen in 161 games. The Giants achieved their mark in 136 games.)

A29   14 hits (September 14, 1913; lost 7–0.

A30   Christy Mathewson (1901)

A31   George "Hooks" Wiltse

A32   47 (April 1913)

A33   Ferdie Schupp defeated Brooklyn 4–1 in the first game, and Rube Benton won the last over the Boston Braves, 4–1

A34   Philadelphia Phillies (September 28, 1919; 6–1); 51 minutes

Q35 In 1933, Carl Hubbell joined the likes of Washington's Walter Johnson (1918), Detroit's Ed Summers (1908), and Providence's John Ward (1882). What record do these pitchers share?

Q36 In 1935, two brothers faced each other as the Giants met the Dodgers on July 5, 1935. It was the first time in major league history that opposing siblings both hit homers. Name the two players.

Q37 The 1947 Giants share the 154-game major league season record for most home runs. How many did the team hit that year, and what other club belted the same number of homers?

Q38 The Giants' Johnny Mize is the only player to share the home run title twice with the same player. Who was his "partner"?

Q39 Willie Mays is one of two men to achieve the following: hit more than 300 home runs and steal more than 300 bases. With whom does Mays share this honor?

Q40 This Giant is one of five men ever to hit 20 doubles, 20 triples, and 20 home runs in the same season. Who was he?

Q41 What Giant holds the record for most career home runs in the same park?

Q42 What Giant was the last National Leaguer to bat .400 in a season?

Q43 The 1947 Giants were led in hitting by a slugger who set a National League standard for home runs in one year by a lefty. Who was he?

Q44 Who was the first National League player to hit 500 home runs?

Q45 What New York Giant leads the team in games (2,730), at-bats (9,456), runs (1,859), hits (2,876), home runs (511), total bases (5,041), and extra-base hits (1,071)?

Q46 Two New York Giants have hit 51 home runs in a season. Name the tandem.

NEW YORK GIANTS

A35   Longest shutout games (each threw for 18 scoreless innings)

A36   Giants: Al Cuccinello; Dodgers: Tony Cuccinello (Brooklyn won 14–4)

A37   221 home runs, a feat matched by the 1956 Cincinnati Reds

A38   Pittsburgh's Ralph Kiner (in 1947 and 1948, Mize and Kiner led the National League with 51 and 40 homers respectively)

A39   Bobby Bonds

A40   Willie Mays (1957) (the others: Cub Frank Schulte, 1911; Cardinal Jim Bottomley, 1928; Indian Jeff Heath, 1941; Royal George Brett, 1979)

A41   Mel Ott (323 home runs in the Polo Grounds; 1926–47)

A42   First baseman Bill Terry (1930: .401)

A43   Johnny Mize (he hit 51 homers and led his team to a major-league-record 221 home runs in a 154-game season)

A44   Mel Ott

A45   Mel Ott

A46   Johnny Mize (1947) and Willie Mays (1955)

New York Mets

NEW YORK METS

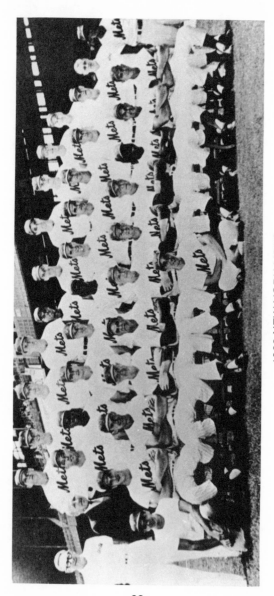

1962 NEW YORK METS

THE SUITS

Q1 President and CEO of the Mets Fred Wilpon pitched batting practice at Ebbets Field for the Brooklyn Dodgers. He was also a high school teammate of a Hall of Fame player. Name his famous friend.

Q2 Davey Johnson has the highest won-loss percentage among Met managers. Who has the lowest?

Q3 What three men have been selected as All-Star managers while piloting the Mets?

Q4 Name the five ballparks Casey Stengel played, managed, or coached in while wearing a uniform from a New York team.

Q5 Casey Stengel was on pennant-winning teams with three New York franchises: as a player with the Dodgers and Giants, and as the manager of the Yankees. How old was Stengel when he became the Mets' manager?

Q6 What three major league teams did Casey Stengel manage before he joined the Mets?

Q7 Rogers Hornsby was a coach with the Mets in the first year of their existence. As a player, he set a number of records that still stand today, including his 1924 batting average, the highest in modern history. What is that mark?

Q8 After he broke his hip, Casey Stengel retired in 1964. Who succeeded him?

NEW YORK METS

A1 Sandy Koufax (while Wilpon pitched, Koufax played first base)

A2 Casey Stengel (won: 175; lost: 404; pct.: .302)

A3 Gil Hodges (1970), Yogi Berra (1974), and Davey Johnson (1987)

A4 Washington Park, Ebbets Field, Polo Grounds, Yankee Stadium, and Shea Stadium

A5 71 years old

A6 Brooklyn Dodgers (1934–36), Boston Braves (1938–43), and Yankees (1949–60)

A7 .424 (established while playing for the St. Louis Cardinals)

A8 Wes Westrum

Q9 In addition to coaching the team, Yogi Berra had a short stint as a player with the Mets in 1965. In how many games did Yogi see action?

Q10 What 1957 Cy Young Award winner was a player-coach with the Mets in 1965?

Q11 Who replaced Yogi Berra when he was given the ax by the Mets in 1975?

Q12 On May 17, 1985, Bud Harrelson was hired as the third-base coach by Davey Johnson. Whom did Harrelson replace on the Mets' staff?

Q13 Davey Johnson has the unique distinction of having batted behind two of baseball's greatest home run hitters. Who were they?

Q14 What major league record does Davey Johnson share with St. Louis's Rogers Hornsby?

Q15 Davey Johnson is the last batter to get a hit off what Hall of Fame pitcher?

Q16 Besides the Mets, with what teams did Bud Harrelson play during his major league career?

Q17 Whose team record did Harrelson tie when he appeared in the Mets' starting lineup for a season opener 11 times?

F.Y.I.

Q18 The Mets' logo was unveiled on November 16, 1961. Name the cartoonist who designed it.

Q19 What other city received a major league baseball franchise the same year as the Mets?

Q20 In a contest to determine the team's name, "Mets" was the winner, with 61 votes. What moniker was second with 47 ballots?

NEW YORK METS

A9 Four (two as catcher and two as a pinch-hitter; after nine at-bats and two singles, he ended his career)

A10 Warren Spahn

A11 Coach Roy McMillan

A12 Bobby Valentine (he left to manage the Texas Rangers)

A13 Atlanta Brave Hank Aaron and Yomiuri Giant Sadaharu Oh (Johnson played two seasons in Japan with the Giants)

A14 Most home runs—42—by a second baseman

A15 Sandy Koufax (Johnson's hit came in Game 2 of the 1966 Series, which Baltimore won, 6–0)

A16 The Philadelphia Phillies (1978 and 1979) and the Texas Rangers (1980)

A17 Tom Seaver

A18 Ray Gatto

A19 Houston (the Colt .45s)

A20 Empires

*** FAST FACTS ***
Mets Managers

		Win/Loss			Win/Loss
1962–65	Casey Stengel	175–404	1976–77	Joe Frazier	101–106
1965–67	Wes Westrum	142–237	1977–81	Joe Torre	286–420
1967	Salty Parker	4–7	1982–83	George Bamberger	81–127
1968–71	Gil Hodges	339–309	1983	Frank Howard	52–64
1972–75	Yogi Berra	292–296	1984–90	Davey Johnson	595–417
1975	Roy McMillan	26–27	1990–	Bud Harrelson	71–49

Q21 Among the names considered for the new National League entry in 1961: the Rebels; Skyliners; NYB's; Burros; Continentals; and Avengers. Two other names eventually appeared on the New York sports scene. What are they?

Q22 The Mets played the Yankees for the first time on March 22, 1962, in St. Petersburg, Florida. What was the outcome of the preseason game?

Q23 The first game played by the Mets in Gotham was on April 13, 1962, at the Polo Grounds. Whom did they meet?

Q24 The Mets opened their first season on the road. Who was their opponent on April 11, 1962?

Q25 Who is the only member of the Mets organization to be with the franchise since its inception in 1962?

Q26 How many consecutive games did the Mets lose at the start of their first season?

Q27 In the Mets' first season, how many games out of first did the team finish?

Q28 How many players started in both the 1962 and 1963 Mets opening game?

Q29 How many ex-Dodgers started the 1963 season for the Mets?

Q30 The last game at the Polo Grounds took place on September 18, 1963. Who was the Mets' opponent, and what was the score?

Q31 The Mets played their first game in Shea Stadium on April 17, 1964. Who was their opponent?

Q32 The first hit in Shea Stadium was also the first home run. Who belted it?

Q33 Whom did the Mets rout in 1964 by a score of 19–1?

Q34 What pitcher threw the first perfect game in the National League since 1880 against the Mets?

NEW YORK METS

A21 The Islanders and Jets

A22 The Mets won, 4–3

A23 Pittsburgh Pirates (Pittsburgh won, 4–3; WP: Tom Sturdivant; LP: Sherman ''Roadblock'' Jones)

A24 St. Louis Cardinals (the Cards won, 11–4; WP: Larry Jackson; LP: Roger Craig; the team's first official game, which was scheduled for April 10 in St. Louis, was rained out)

A25 Head grounds keeper Pete Flynn (Flynn started as a member of the grounds crew in 1962 and was promoted to his present position in 1974)

A26 They lost nine straight before defeating the Pirates in Pittsburgh on April 23 (score: 10–1; WP: Jay Hook; LP: Tom Sturdivant)

A27 60 1/2 games behind first-place teams L.A. and San Francisco (their record was 40–120)

A28 Two (OF Frank Thomas and IF Charlie Neal—Neal was switched from second base to third base)

A29 Five (1B Tim Harkness, 2B Larry Burright, 3B Charlie Neal, OF Duke Snider, P Roger Craig)

A30 The Philadelphia Phillies defeated New York, 5–1

A31 Pittsburgh Pirates (Pirates won, 4–3, behind the pitching of Bob Friend; the losing pitcher was Ed Bauta)

A32 Willie Stargell (in the second inning off Met Dick Ellsworth)

A33 Chicago Cubs (May 26, 1964)

A34 Philadelphia's Jim Bunning (on Father's Day, June 21, 1964)

Q35 On May 31, 1964, the Mets played a doubleheader that resulted in the longest day in baseball history. Among the major league records set: most innings one day (32), longest game (7:23), and longest doubleheader (9:52). Who was the Mets' opponent?

Q36 Which of the following did NOT occur in the marathon doubleheader of May 31, 1964?

    (a) home plate was stolen
    (b) there was a triple play executed
    (c) Willie Mays played shortstop
    (d) every player got a hit

Q37 On August 26, 1965, the Mets finally beat Dodger Sandy Koufax, behind the pitching of rookie Tug McGraw. How many times had Koufax defeated New York up until that point?

Q38 When did the Mets finish out of the NL cellar for the first time?

Q39 In what position did the Mets finish the season in 1968, the year before they became world champs?

Q40 What opposing pitcher struck out 19 Mets in one game during the 1969 season, but lost to New York, 4–3?

Q41 Whom did the Mets defeat in a 1969 doubleheader to reach first place for the first time in their history?

Q42 In what year did the Mets win their first opening day game?

Q43 The Mets and umpire Ed Sudol have quite a history together. For which event was Sudol NOT umpiring a Mets game?

    (a) The Mets' first game ever
    (b) Mets' first home-opener victory
    (c) All three 20-plus inning games the Mets played in their history
    (d) The Mets' final-game victories in the 1969 and 1973 NL Championships

Q44 There have been 12 inside-the-park home runs at Shea, including Cardinal Terry Pendleton's on June 6, 1985. What was unique about Pendleton's tater?

Q45 In 1985, the Mets were eliminated from the NL East title in the next-to-last game of the season. Who nipped them for the championship?

NEW YORK METS

A35 San Francisco Giants (the Giants won the opener, 5–3, in regulation and the nightcap marathon, 6–4, in 23 innings)

A36 (d) (Giant Orlando Cepeda stole home, Met shortstop Roy McMillan engineered a triple play, and Mays played three innings at short)

A37 13 times (he gave up only 15 earned runs in the process, including a no-hitter on June 30, 1962)

A38 1966 (with a record of 66–95, they finished 28 1/2 games out of first, but passed Chicago to end up in ninth place)

A39 Ninth place (with a record of 73–89, they finished the closest to first place up until that point by being 24 games out)

A40 Cardinal Steve Carlton (in surrendering only two hits, Carlton lost because of Ron Swoboda's two two-run homers)

A41 Montreal Expos (they beat them 3–2 and 7–1 to overtake the Chicago Cubs by .001 on September 10)

A42 1970 (at Pittsburgh: 5–3, in 11 innings)

A43 (b)

A44 It was a grand slam home run (off pitcher Joe Sambito)

A45 St. Louis Cardinals (despite winning four times in six games against the Cards that September, the Mets coud not make up enough ground)

Q46 What three uniform numbers have been retired by the Mets?

Q47 Name the club the Mets have defeated the most times in their history.

Q48 Which opposing pitcher has won the most games against the Mets?

Q49 The club record for consecutive wins is eight and is held by two players. Who are they?

Q50 What pitcher holds the team record for highest winning percentage in a season with .870?

Q51 How many Mets have thrown a no-hitter?

Q52 Only twice in team history have Mets pitchers hit grand slam home runs. Name the two hurlers.

Q53 Which Mets pitcher has hit the most home runs?

Q54 Only two Mets have ever won the Cy Young Award—Tom Seaver and Dwight Gooden. Which player was younger at the time he captured the award?

Q55 Who was the only pitcher with a winning record on the Mets' 1962 team?

Q56 When Roger Craig lost 18 straight games in 1963 (April 29 to August 9), he fell one game short of the major league record. Who set the mark with 19 consecutive losses?

Q57 While in the twilight of his playing days (April 1965), Warren Spahn struck out the 2,500th player of his career as a Met. Who was in the box against Spahn?

Q58 In 1967, Jerry Koosman tied a 63-year-old record for rookies when he won 19 games (with an ERA of 2.08), and he was second in Rookie of the Year balloting by a single vote. Who edged Koosman for the honor that year?

NEW YORK METS

A46   Nos. 37 (Casey Stengel), 14 (Gil Hodges), and 41 (Tom Seaver)

A47   Chicago Cubs

A48   Steve Carlton (30 wins; he also has 36 defeats at the hands of the Mets)

A49   Tom Seaver (1969) and David Cone (1988)

A50   David Cone (1988; he bettered Dwight Gooden's .857, set in 1985)

A51   None (there have been 17 one-hitters, including five by Seaver and two by Jon Matlack)

A52   Carl Willey (July 15, 1963: against Houston) and Jack Hamilton (May 20, 1967: against St. Louis)

A53   Tom Seaver (6)

A54   Gooden—20 years old (Seaver, a three-time winner, his first won at age 24)

A55   Ken McKenzie (5–4)

A56   Philadelphia A's John Nabors (1916)

A57   Spahn struck out Dodger rookie Jim LeFebvre

A58   Cincinnati's Johnny Bench

Q59 Roberto Clemente got his 3,000th (and final) hit off a Met. Name the pitcher involved.

Q60 Pete Rose surpassed Tommy Holmes's 37-game National League record for consecutive hits by belting a single on July 25, 1978, against New York. Who served up the record pitch?

Q61 In May 1981, Yale's Ron Darling threw 11 innings of no-hit ball against St. John's University in an NCAA regional playoff game, but wound up losing, 1–0, in 12 innings. What pitcher, and future Mets teammate, was credited with the win?

Q62 The only Met batter never to make an out, this pitcher appeared in 26 games and posted a 1.000 winning record (1–0), had one save, and a batting average of 1.000 (1 for 1). Name the "perfect player."

Q63 Name the three pitchers who have won both ends of a Met doubleheader.

Q64 What three uniform numbers has Ron Darling worn with the Mets?

Q65 The first time that Cy Young Award winners from the previous year met in a regular-season game occurred on August 28, 1989. What two pitchers faced off in the contest?

—THE FRANCHISE—

Q66 Seaver ended his career with a 311–205 record, and an ERA of 2.86. What three modern-day major league pitchers have a better ERA? (minimum: 3,000 innings)

Q67 One of the many records Seaver established is consecutive seasons with 200 or more strikeouts. How many did he have?

Q68 How many times was Seaver a Cy Young Award winner?

Q69 How many times was Seaver named to the All-Star squad?

Q70 What two pitchers have more career strikeouts than Tom Seaver?

NEW YORK METS

A59   Jon Matlock (September 30, 1972; he gave up a double to Clemente in the fourth inning)

A60   Craig Swan (though Rose had hit in his 38th straight game, the Mets won the game, 9–2)

A61   Frank Viola (Darling's game is still the longest no-hitter in NCAA tournament history)

A62   Ray Searage (1981)

A63   Craig Anderson (1962), Willard Hunter (1964), and Jesse Orosco (1983)

A64   44, 12, and 15

A65   Frank Viola and L.A.'s Orel Hershiser (Viola won the match, 1–0, by tossing a three-hitter. Viola had won the award in 1988 while with Minnesota.)

_____ . _____

A66   Walter Johnson (2.37), Glover Cleveland Alexander (2.56), and Whitey Ford (2.74)

A67   Nine (from 1968 through 1976)

A68   Three (1969, 1973, and 1975)

A69   12 times (all with the National League)

A70   Nolan Ryan and Steve Carlton

THE UNIFORMS

Q71 Seaver's first, 1,000th, 2,000th, and 3,000th strikeout victims were Pirate Donn Clendenon (1967), Philly Willie Montanez (1971), Red Danny Driessen (1975), and Card Keith Hernandez (1981). What else do these players have in common?

Q72 What do Jimmy Qualls and Joe Wallis of the Cubs and Leron Lee of the Padres have in common?

Q73 Tom Seaver holds the record for most opening-day starts. What is it?

Q74 Name the big-league team Tom Terrific never defeated.

Q75 What major league first was established when Tom Seaver won his Rookie of the Year Award in 1967?

Q76 What is Tom Seaver's record for striking out consecutive batters?

Q77 In his first game after the Mets traded him, Seaver pitched a six-hitter against his former team. Who was on the New York mound in the Mets' 5–1 loss to the Reds?

Q78 Cincinnati sent four players to New York for pitcher Tom Seaver on June 15, 1977. Name them.

Q79 Seaver was the Mets' starter in every opening day lineup from 1968 to 1977. Name the opening day pitchers for the 1967 season and the 1978 season.

Q80 When Seaver arrived in Cincinnati, who relinquished number 41 so the former Met could don the uniform he had worn for the previous 101/2 seasons?

Q81 Tom Seaver didn't throw his first no-hitter until June 16, 1978, while with Cincinnati. What team did he victimize?

Q82 In what year did Tom Terrific experience his first losing season?

Q83 The Mets reacquired Seaver in December 1982. Whom did they trade for the man they once called "the Franchise"?

Q84 On August 4, 1985, Seaver pitched his 300th career victory. What team did he defeat that day?

NEW YORK METS

A71 All played first base

A72 All three players broke up potential no-hitters by Seaver (the hits all came in the ninth inning)

A73 Sixteen games in which he started the season

A74 Toronto Blue Jays

A75 It was the first time the award was given to a player from a last-place team

A76 10 (April 22, 1970: against San Diego Padres)

A77 Jerry Koosman

A78 Infielder Doug Flynn, pitcher Pat Zachry, outfielder Dan Norman, and outfielder Steve Henderson

A79 1967: Don Cardwell; 1978: Jerry Koosman

A80 Joe Nuxhall

A81 St. Louis Cardinals

A82 1982: 5–13 (his 16th season in the majors and his sixth with Cincinnati)

A83 Charlie Puleo, Lloyd McClendon, and Jason Felice

A84 The Yankees (Seaver's victory was registered in New York on "Phil Rizzuto Day" while Tom was throwing for the White Sox)

Q85 On the same day Seaver recorded his 300th win, what major league player got his 3,000th hit?

Q86 On August 17, 1986, Seaver recorded his final career victory, number 311. Whom did he defeat?

_____ · _____

Q87 Nolan Ryan, one of the greatest pitchers of all time, was a Met for five seasons (1966, 1968–71). To whom and for what was he traded?

Q88 Nolan Ryan's 300th win came on July 31, 1990, in an 11–3 Texas victory over Milwaukee. Who was the last pitcher before Ryan to reach the 300 plateau?

Q89 How many no-hitters has ex-Met Nolan Ryan pitched in his career?

Q90 For what distinction is Dwight (Doc) Gooden noted in All-Star competition?

Q91 Which of these records did Dwight Gooden NOT establish?

   (a) Major league mark for rookie strikeouts, 18, in a game
   (b) Major league record with 43 strikeouts in three
       consecutive games
   (c) Major league record with an average of 11.39 strikeouts
       per nine innings
   (d) Only major league pitcher to strike out 200-plus in each
       of his first three seasons

Q92 Name the four Mets who have won Rookie of the Year honors while playing with New York.

Q93 What do the following players have in common: Doc Medich, Robert L. Gibson, Luis Alvarado, Francisco Estrada, and Mac Scarce?

Q94 The Mets have had the No. 1 overall pick in the amateur draft four times. Whom did they select with those choices?

Q95 Who was the Mets' first selection in the 1961 National League expansion draft?

NEW YORK METS

A85 Rod Carew

A86 Minnesota Twins (in the Metrodome)

———————————— · ————————————

A87 He was traded to the California Angels (along with Lee Stanton, Don Rose, and Francisco Estrada) for Jim Fregosi (December 10, 1971)

A88 Don Sutton (June 1986)

A89 Six (a major league record; he never threw one while with New York)

A90 At 19 years, 7 months, and 24 days, he was the youngest player to appear in an All-Star game (July 10, 1984)

A91 (a)—Gooden struck out 16 in a game in his rookie season, two short of the all-time mark of 18 set by Montreal's Bill Gullickson

A92 Tom Seaver (1967), Jon Matlock (1972), Darryl Strawberry (1983), and Dwight Gooden (1984)

A93 They have played in one and only one regular-season game for the Mets

A94 1966: C Steve Chilcott; 1968: IF Tim Foli; 1980: OF Darryl Strawberry; 1984: OF Shawn Abner

A95 Catcher Hobie Landrith (from San Francisco)

Q12. On May 17, 1985, Bud Harrelson was hired as the third-base coach by Davey Johnson. What former Met (above) did he replace?

NEW YORK METS

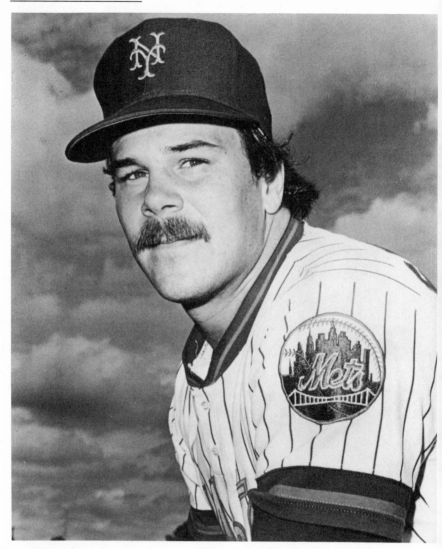

Q62. The only Met batter never to make an out, this pitcher appeared in 26 games and posted a 1.000 winning record (1-0), had one save, and a batting average of 1.000 (1 for 1). Name this "perfect player."

Q109. On May 15, 1962, Marv Throneberry (above) played in his first Met game. Whom did he replace at first base on that day?

NEW YORK METS

Q167. Who leads the Mets with five grand slam home runs?

Q96 The team's first recorded home run came in its inaugural game on April 11, 1962. Who belted it?

Q97 What three players from the original 1962 Mets would go on to become major league managers?

Q98 The only time in major league history that one team had two players with identical first and last names occurred in 1962. Who are they?

Q99 The youngest Met to appear in a game was 17 years, 10 months, and 14 days old when he played on September 22, 1962. Name him.

Q100 Who was the first Met selected to the All-Star Game?

Q101 On September 30, 1962, catcher Joe Pignatano hit into a triple play with Sammy Drake on second base and Richie Ashburn on first. Why was the play significant in the major league careers of all three Mets?

Q102 Who was the last Met from the 1962 season to retire/leave the club?

—MARVELOUS MARV—

Q103 What number did Marv Throneberry wear?

Q104 In 1952, Marvelous Marv inked a bonus contract with a major league club right out of high school. What team signed him?

Q105 First base was not always Throneberry's regular position. Where did he start his career, and after what Hall of Famer did he fashion himself?

Q106 Marv won four minor league home run titles before his 25th birthday, but never got a shot with the parent club because another player, who preceded him by only a year, was already with the majors. Who "displaced" Marv?

Q107 When Throneberry was traded by the Yankees to Kansas City in 1959, what A's players came to New York?

Q108 From what team did the Mets acquire Marvelous Marv in 1962?

Q109 On May 15, 1962, Marv Throneberry played in his first Met game. Whom did he replace at first base on that date?

NEW YORK METS

A96 Gil Hodges

A97 Don Zimmer, Roger Craig, and Gil Hodges

A98 Robert L. Miller (pitcher: 1962, 1973–74) and Robert G. Miller (pitcher: 1962) (both were called Bob)

A99 Ed Kranepool

A100 Richie Ashburn (OF, 1962; he sat on the bench for the whole game)

A101 It was the last major league at-bat for the three players

A102 Ed Kranepool (he called it quits in 1979)

A103 No. 2

A104 New York Yankees

A105 Outfield; Mickey Mantle

A106 Bill Skowron

A107 Roger Maris, Joe DeMaestri, and Kent Hadley (Hank Bauer, Don Larsen, and Norm Siebern were also swapped to K.C.)

A108 Baltimore Orioles (for Hobie Landrith and $40,000)

A109 Hall of Famer Gil Hodges

Q110 In a Marvelous Marv classic, Throneberry hit a triple against the Cubs, which drove in two runs and might have won New York the game except that Marv was ejected before the next pitch was even tossed. What happened?

Q111 In 1962, Throneberry had his best major league season and was one of the Mets' most productive hitters. What was his average?

Q112 How long did Throneberry, who epitomized the Mets' ineptitude, play for New York?

Q113 Who was the last player to hit a home run at the Polo Grounds?

Q114 In 1963, second baseman Ron Hunt was runner up in Rookie of the Year balloting. Who won the honor that year?

Q115 In 1963, Jimmy Piersall was purchased from the Washington Senators. He was released after only 40 games (he was batting .194) but not before he hit the 100th home run of his career at the Polo Grounds. How did Piersall celebrate the milestone?

Q116 What pitcher gave up Jimmy Piersall's 100th home run?

Q117 In June 1965, baseball's first free-agent draft took place. Whom did the Mets select?

Q118 What longtime Met was signed by the team in 1965 on the recommendation of a Shea Stadium usher?

Q119 The Mets had the opportunity to select Reggie Jackson in the 1966 draft with the first pick overall, but they passed on him. Whom did they choose instead?

Q120 Who was the leading hitter for the 1969 Mets?

Q121 What first-round draft choice of the Mets did not sign with the team?

NEW YORK METS

A110 Ernie Banks called for the ball and touched first base, and the ump called Throneberry out for missing the bag (As Stengel rushed out to dispute the call, the first-base coach stopped him cold when he informed Casey that Marv had missed second base as well. Charlie Neal followed Marv's blunder with a home run. The Mets lost 8–7. Had Throneberry been on third base, New York could have tied the game.)

A111 .244 (with 16 homers and 49 RBIs in 116 games)

A112 Two seasons (in 1962, he was with the team for 116 games; in 1963, he was expendable after 14 at-bats and was optioned to Triple-A Buffalo)

_____ · _____

A113 Met Jim Hickman (September 18, 1963)

A114 Cincinnati's Pete Rose

A115 He ran backwards around the bases (in sequence). It was Piersall's only National League home run.

A116 Philly's Dallas Green

A117 Les Rohr (the pitcher never played in an major league game)

A118 Jerry Koosman

A119 Steve Chilcott (Chilcott never played a game in the majors)

A120 Cleon Jones (.340 average, 164 hits, and 12 home runs)

A121 1970 shortstop George Ambrow (After leaving high school, he opted to play at USC. Ambrow injured his knees and never played in the big leagues.)

Q122 On May 14, 1972, Willie Mays debuted with the Mets and hit a fifth-inning home run that won the game. Whom did New York defeat that day?

Q123 Whom did the Mets send to San Francisco on May 11, 1972, in return for Willie Mays?

Q124 What Met popularized the rallying cry "You Gotta Believe" in 1973?

Q125 What NFL team drafted catcher John Stearns?

Q126 In 1978, Jerry Koosman spent his last season with the team before being sent to Minnesota. Whom did the Twins give up to obtain Koos?

Q127 One-time Met Ellis Vallentine (1981–82) once attempted to escape a rundown while caught between first and second base. What did he try?

Q128 Ron Darling was obtained with pitcher Walt Terrell from Texas. Whom did the Mets send to the Rangers?

Q129 Met Tim Teufel was drafted three times in his amateur career. What teams selected him?

Q130 The first trade between the Yankees and the Mets involving major league players took place on December 11, 1987. What two Mets were sent across town for Phil Lombardi, Darren Reed, and Steve Frey?

Q131 David Cone was obtained from Kansas City in 1987 for catcher Ed Hearn and pitchers Rick Anderson and Mauro Gozzo. Name the player who also came to New York in the deal.

Q132 How many times has Darryl Strawberry hit a home run in his first at-bat of the year?

Q133 Howard Johnson became the third player in the majors to hit 30 home runs and steal 30 bases in a single season more than once in his career. Name the other two.

Q134 Mike Marshall was obtained from the Dodgers along with Alejandro Peña for what Met?

NEW YORK METS

A122 San Francisco Giants (the same team that traded the 41-year-old star to the Mets only three days before)

A123 Pitcher Charlie Williams

A124 Tug McGraw

A125 Buffalo Bills

A126 Jesse Orosco and Greg Field

A127 He called time-out (it didn't work; a request for time-out must be preceded or succeeded by a play, but cannot occur in the middle of one)

A128 Lee Mazzilli

A129 Milwaukee (1978), Chicago White Sox (1979), and Minnesota (1980) (after passing the first two times, he finally signed with the Twins)

A130 Rafael Santana and Victor Garcia (the first exchange of players involved minor leaguers—IF Roy Staiger went to the Yankees for IF Sergio Ferrer; December 9, 1977)

A131 Catcher Chris Jelic

A132 Three (1984, 1987, 1988)

A133 Bobby Bonds (who accomplished the feat five times) and Willie Mays (twice)

A134 Juan Samuel

THE UNIFORMS

Q135 What player hit three home runs in a game twice in his career—once while playing for the Mets, the other while playing against the Mets?

GLORY DAYS

Q136 Which starting pitcher has posted the lowest ERA in a Met World Series?

Q137 What player registered the first postseason home run for the Mets?

Q138 Whom did the Mets defeat in 1969 to win the National League pennant?

Q139 Who hit a home run in each of the three games in the 1969 NL Championship Series?

Q140 What pitching tandem combined to shut out the Orioles in Game 3 of the 1969 World Series?

Q141 Who was the Mets' starting pitcher in the fifth (and final) game of the 1969 Series?

Q142 After spotting the Orioles three runs (on dingers by Dave McNally and Frank Robinson) in Game 5, the Mets came back with home runs by Donn Clendenon and Al Weis. Who had the winning RBI in the Mets' 5–3 victory?

Q143 Who made the last out in the 1969 World Series?

Q144 In 1973, the Mets clinched the NL East title on the last day of the season. Whom did New York defeat on October 1?

Q145 In the opening game of the 1973 NL Championship Series, the Mets lost by a score of 2–1. Who drove in the team's only run?

Q146 The third game of the NL Championship Series was marred by a bench-clearing brawl in the ninth inning. What two players provoked the fracas?

NEW YORK METS

A135 Dave Kingman (he was with the Chicago Cubs the second time)

_____ . _____

A136 Ron Darling (1986: 1.53 in three starts)

A137 Tommie Agee (1969 NL championship series; Game 2)

A138 Atlanta Braves (the Mets beat them three straight in a best-of-five series)

A139 Atlanta's Hank Aaron

A140 Gary Gentry and reliever Nolan Ryan

A141 Jerry Koosman

A142 Ron Swoboda (with Eddie Watt pitching, Swoboda hit a double down the left-field line to score Cleon Jones from second base)

A143 Baltimore second baseman Davey Johnson

A144 Chicago Cubs (5–4) (on August 30, the Mets were in last place; by September 21, they had climbed into first and eventually won 23 of their last 32 games)

A145 Tom Seaver (his double drove in Bud Harrelson)

A146 Bud Harrelson and Pete Rose (Rose was attempting to break up a double play and slid hard into Harrelson)

Q147 What Red hit a home run in the 12th inning of the fourth game to force the 1973 National League Series to five games?

Q148 Who are the only Mets to play in all 12 of the club's 1969 and 1973 World Series games?

Q149 Game 2 of the 1973 fall classic was the longest contest in World Series history in terms of time—4:13. Who put New York in the lead in the 12th inning?

Q150 Whose errors allowed the Mets to score three unearned runs in the 12th inning and an eventual 10–7 victory in Game 2 in 1973?

Q151 New York jumped to a 3–2 Series lead before eventually bowing in seven games. Who was the Mets' leading hitter, with 11 hits, six RBIs, and a .423 Series batting average?

Q152 In the 1986 NL Championship Series, the sixth and final game went 16 innings—the longest postseason game in major league history. Who scored the winning run in that game?

Q153 Who won the MVP award for the 1986 NL Championship Series?

Q154 The Mets lost the first two games of the 1986 World Series at home but came back to win the championship, four games to three. Name the only other team to accomplish this.

Q155 The only score of Game 1 in the 1986 Series came with Jim Rice on second base in the seventh inning. Rice scored on a muffed grounder. Name the player who hit the ball and the player responsible for the error.

Q156 In Game 3 of the 1986 Series, what Met became the 14th player in major league history to lead off a Series game with a home run?

Q157 Going into the eighth inning of Game 6, the score was 3–2, with Boston ahead. Who drove in the tying run for the Mets in the bottom of the eighth, and who crossed the plate?

Q158 The score was tied at 3–3 in the top of the 10th when two Sox scored to put Boston in the lead. Name the scorers.

Q159 Before the Mets began their rally in the 10th inning, they had two outs against them. Who put the team in the hole?

NEW YORK METS

A147 Pete Rose (off loser Harry Parker)

A148 Jerry Grote, Bud Harrelson, and Cleon Jones

A149 Willie Mays (his single put the Mets ahead 7–6; it was the last hit of his 22-year career)

A150 Mike Andrews of the A's (Owner Charlie Finley deactivated Andrews after the game, but Commissioner Bowie Kuhn ordered that the player be reinstated.)

A151 Rusty Staub

A152 Wally Backman, who was singled in by Len Dykstra

A153 Houston's Mike Scott (in 18 innings, Scott gave up eight hits and one run, for a .050 ERA)

A154 The 1985 Kansas City Royals (against the St. Louis Cardinals)

A155 Rich Gedman's grounder was booted by Tim Teufel

A156 Len Dykstra (off Dennis Boyd)

A157 Gary Carter hit a 3–0 pitch and sacrificed to allow Lee Mazzilli to score

A158 Dave Henderson hit a home run and Wade Boggs, who hit a double, came home on Marty Barrett's single.

A159 Wally Backman flied out to Jim Rice and Keith Hernandez flied out to Dave Henderson

Q160 What three Mets got consecutive hits to put New York in a position to win the game?

Q161 Boston's Calvin Schiraldi was relieved in the 10th after pitching 1 2/3 innings. Schiraldi's replacement threw a wild pitch, which allowed Kevin Mitchell to score the tying run. Who was the pitcher?

Q162 Who grounded the ball through Bill Buckner's legs?

SETTING THE STANDARD

Q163 What are the most consecutive victories the Mets have had?

Q164 Which Met has played the most games at any one position?

Q165 Who holds the club record for hitting in consecutive games?

Q166 The club record for consecutive games with a home run is four and is held by a quartet of players. Name the Mets tied for the record.

Q167 Who leads the Mets with five grand slam home runs?

Q168 Which outfielder has the Mets' best single-season fielding average in his position (minimum: 100 games)?

Q169 This Met holds the major league home run record for an expansion team's inaugural season. Name the player.

Q170 Who is the club's all-time team leader in hit-by-pitches with 41?

Q171 In the same game that Tom Seaver set two major league standards—striking out 19 and striking out 10 straight batters—his catcher also established a record with 20 putouts. Who is he?

Q172 The most runs ever registered by the Mets in one inning came at the expense of Cincinnati on June 12, 1972. How many did they score in their record-breaking sixth inning?

NEW YORK METS

A160 Gary Carter (lined a 2–1 pitch to left field); Kevin Mitchell (batting for Rick Aguilera, lined a 0–1 pitch to center field); Ray Knight (looped a 0–2 pitch to center, and Carter scored, Mitchell going to third)

A161 Bob Stanley

A162 Mookie Wilson (off of the 10th pitch by Stanley and with the count at 3–2; Ray Knight scored the winning run)

———————————— · ————————————

A163 11 (they accomplished the feat four times: 1969, 1972, 1986, and 1990)

A164 Ed Kranepool (1B, 1,304 games) (other position leaders—2B: Wally Backman, 680; SS: Bud Harrelson, 1,281; C: Jerry Grote, 1,176; OF: Cleon Jones, 1,103; 3B: Howard Johnson, still active)

A165 Hubie Brooks (1984: 24 games)

A166 Dave Kingman (1981), Ron Swoboda (1968), Lee Mazzilli (1980), and Larry Elliot (1964)

A167 John Milner (1971–77)

A168 Len Dykstra (1988: .996) (Other bests—1B Ed Kranepool, 1971: .998; 2B Ken Boswell, 1970: .996; SS Bud Harrelson, 1973: .979; 3B Len Randle, 1978: .967; C Mike Fitzgerald, 1984: .994; P Gary Gentry, 1969: 1.000)

A169 Frank Thomas (34 homers)

A170 Ron Hunt

A171 Jerry Grote (he surpassed L.A.'s John Roseboro and Detroit's Bill Freehan, who were tied with 19)

A172 10 runs (the Mets won the game, 12–6)

Q173 What Met is the only major league player to collect at least 500 hits for four different clubs?

Q174 What Met holds the National League record for single-season homers by a switch hitter?

Q175 Kevin McReynolds set a major league record in 1988 for most stolen bases without being caught in a season. What is his record, and whose mark did he eclipse?

Q176 Mark Carreon tied a Met record in 1989 when he hit four pinch-hit home runs. Whose record did he match?

Q177 On August 1, 1990, the Mets used a pitcher to pinch-hit in a game and he pinch-hit safely—a first for the franchise. Name the hurler.

Q178 Who holds the record for most home runs by an opposing player against the Mets?

NEW YORK METS

A173 Rusty Staub (he did it with the Astros, Expos, Tigers, and Mets)

A174 Howard Johnson (1987: 36 home runs)

A175 His 21 consecutive steals broke the record held by Oakland's Jimmy Sexton in 1982

A176 Danny Heep's (1983)

A177 David Cone (he hit a single in the 12th inning against the Expos and the Mets won, 6–4)

A178 Willie Stargell (59 home runs)

*** FAST FACTS ***

Mets Seasonal Records

Games: Felix Millan, 162 (1975)
At-Bats: Felix Millan, 676 (1975)
Hits: Felix Millan, 191 (1975)
Doubles: Howard Johnson, 41 (1989)
Triples: Mookie Wilson, 10 (1984)
Home Runs: Darryl Strawberry, 39 (1987 and 1988)
Runs: Darryl Strawberry, 108 (1987)
Runs Batted In: Gary Carter, 105 (1986)
Total Bases: Howard Johnson, 319 (1989)
Extra Base Hits: Howard Johnson, 80 (1989)
Batting Average (min: 502 plate appearances): Cleon Jones, .340 (1969)
Slugging Pct. (min: 502 plate appearances): Darryl Strawberry, .583 (1983)
Walks: Darryl Strawberry, 97 (1987)
Stolen Bases: Mookie Wilson, 58 (1982)

New York Knicks

NEW YORK KNICKS

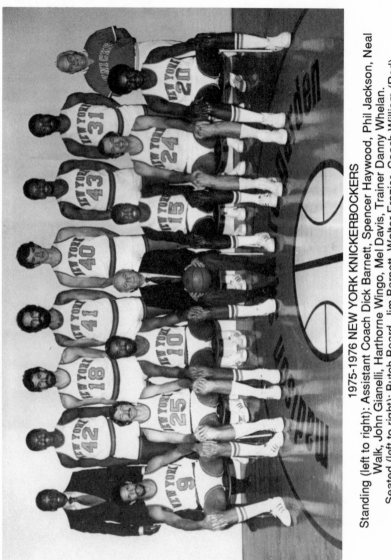

1975-1976 NEW YORK KNICKERBOCKERS
Standing (left to right): Assistant Coach Dick Barnett, Spencer Haywood, Phil Jackson, Neal Walk, John Gianelli, Harthorne Wingo, Mel Davis, Trainer Danny Whelan.
Seated (left to right): Butch Beard, Jim Barnett, Walter Frazier, Coach William (Red) Holzman. Earl Monroe, Bill Bradley, Eugene Short

Q1   Who is the founding father of the New York Knicks?

Q2   There have been seven midseason coaching changes in Knick history. Name the coaches involved.

Q3   Red Holzman had the longest tenure as head coach of the Knicks (14 seasons and 1,097 games). Who has had the shortest?

Q4   For what team did 5'10" floor general William (Red) Holzman play most of his professional career?

Q5   Dick McGuire served as the Knicks' head coach for one-and-a-half years, succeeding Harry Gallatin in 1965. With what other team did McGuire hold the same position?

Q6   What two front office managers switched jobs during the 1967/68 season?

Q7   How many league championships did the Knicks capture under Red Holzman's tutelage?

Q8   What Hall of Fame player was a teammate of Rick Pitino during his college days?

Q9   When Stu Jackson was named coach on July 10, 1989, he was 33 years old. Did that qualify him as the youngest skipper in the NBA?

Q10   Former skipper Stu Jackson was one of the original "Kamikaze Kids" for the Oregon Ducks in the mid-1970s. What NBA head coach did Jackson play under in college?

Q11   Name the two NBA teams John MacLeod coached before he replaced Stu Jackson in December 1990.

Q12   Assistant coach Ernie Grunfeld teamed with former Knick Bernard King to produce "the Bernie & Ernie Show" at their alma mater. Name the school.

Q13   Assistant coach Paul Silas played on 14 playoff teams in 16 NBA seasons, and won three championships. With what two teams did he win the NBA title?

Q14   Paul Silas was the head coach for an NBA team. Name that club.

NEW YORK KNICKS

A1   Ned Irish

A2   1955–56: Joe Lapchick/Vince Boryla; 1959–60: Fuzzy Levane/Carl Braun; 1964–65: Eddie Donovan/Harry Gallatin; 1965–66: Harry Gallatin/Dick McGuire; 1967–68: Dick McGuire/Red Holzman; 1978–79: Willis Reed/Red Holzman; 1986–87: Hubie Brown/Bob Hill

A3   Bob Hill (1986–87: 66 games)

A4   Rochester Royals (he played with the team from 1946 to 1953; his last year was spent with Milwaukee, 1953–54)

A5   Detroit Pistons

A6   Head coach Dick McGuire and chief scout Red Holzman traded places; Red became coach and McGuire became chief scout and assistant coach

A7   Two (1969–70 and 1972–73)

A8   Julius Erving (University of Massachusetts)

A9   Yes

A10   Dick Harter (of the Charlotte Hornets)

A11   Phoenix (1973–74, 1986–87) and Dallas (1987–88, 1989–90)

A12   University of Tennessee

A13   Boston (1973–74 and 1975–76) and Seattle (1978–79)

A14   San Diego Clippers (1980–81 through 1982–83)

Q15   The Knicks are one of two original NBA franchises still in their city of origin. What is the other?

Q16   How many times has the All-Star Game been played at Madison Square Garden?

Q17   What were the Knickerbockers' original colors?

Q18   What was the last year that the Knicks played at the 69th Regiment Armory?

Q19   Whom did the Knicks meet in their last game at the Armory?

Q20   Who made the last basket at the 49th Street Garden?

Q21   Two Knick games were postponed during the 1965–66 season. The December 4th game against Philadelphia was delayed due to the death of the 76er's owner, Ike Richman. Why was the November 9th game put off?

Q22   The Knicks were one of the original 11 members of the Basketball Association of America in 1946 (the forerunner to the NBA). Only three teams still exist. Name the other two.

Q23   Name the present-day sportscaster who was the Knicks' ball boy in 1946 and a clerk for the Brooklyn Dodgers in the same year.

Q24   The Knicks' first radio broadcast was on November 7, 1946, at St. Louis (it was the third game of the season). Name the two announcers who broadcast New York's victory over the Bombers.

Q25   The Knicks' first game (November 1, 1946) was also the league opener. Who was their opponent?

Q26   March 2, 1962: 76er Wilt Chamberlain scored 100 points on 36 field goals and 28 free throws (all records) against New York. Where was the milestone game played?

NEW YORK KNICKS

A15   Boston Celtics

A16   Three times (1954, 1955, and 1968)

A17   Blue, orange, and white (the same as today)

A18   1960 (January 16)

A19   Cincinnati Royals (New York won, 132–106)

A20   Dick Barnett (FG with :05 left against Philadelphia)

A21   Due to the Great Blackout, which hit New York that evening

A22   Boston Celtics and Golden State Warriors (in 1946, the Warriors were located in Philadelphia; they moved to San Francisco and eventually landed in their present locale of Oakland)

A23   Marv Albert

A24   Marty Glickman and Sarah Palfrey Cook (Station WHN)

A25   Toronto Huskies (New York won, 68–66, in Toronto)

A26   Hershey, PA (Philly won, 169–147)

Q27 In one of the club's most memorable games, New York scored the last 19 points of the game in the final five-and-a-half minutes to pull out an 87–86 victory in November 1972. Whom did they meet that night at the Garden?

Q28 Who was the first Knick named league MVP?

Q29 Name the two father-and-son combinations who have played for the Knicks.

Q30 Who was the Knicks' first NBA Rookie of the Year?

Q31 Who hit the Knicks' first three-point basket?

Q32 Who registered the franchise's 15,000th point in a game against New Orleans on October 27, 1977?

Q33 There have been two four-point plays registered against the Knicks (a three-point basket plus a foul and subsequent free throw). The same Knick was called for the foul on both plays. Name him.

Q34 What do Joe Colone, Leo Gottlieb, Bob Knight, John Murphy, and Connie Simmons have in common?

Q35 Whose uniform number was the first to be retired by the Knicks?

Q36 Who was the first Knick to lay claim to the NBA scoring title?

Q37 Which Knick was selected the most times to the NBA All-Defensive team?

Q38 During the 1977–78 season, two Rhodes Scholars were playing for the Knicks. Bill Bradley was one. Who was the other?

Q39 What three Knicks have been chosen NBA Rookie of the Year?

Q40 Who was the first Knick to wear No. 13?

Q41 What Knick won four championships in a row—three NCAA titles and one NBA crown?

NEW YORK KNICKS

A27   Milwaukee Bucks

A28   Willis Reed (1969–70)

A29   Al and Allie McGuire, Ernie and Kiki Vandeweghe

A30   Willis Reed (1964–65 season)

A31   Dave DeBusschere (September 18, 1971: against the Utah ABA Stars at Salt Lake City; it was an exhibition game)

A32   Earl Monroe (the Knicks lost, 123–106)

A33   Micheal Ray Richardson (January 22, 1981: against San Diego's Freeman Williams; March 21, 1982: against Washington's Kevin Grevey)

A34   They did not attend college

A35   Willis Reed (No. 19 was retired in 1976)

A36   Bernard King (1984–85: 32.9 points/game)

A37   Walt Frazier (seven times: 1968–69 through 1974–75)

A38   Forward Tom McMillen

A39   Willis Reed (1964–65), Patrick Ewing (1985–86), Mark Jackson (1987–88)

A40   Ray Williams (1977)

A41   Henry Bibby (1970, 1971, and 1972: UCLA; 1973: New York Knicks)

Q42 Who is the only Knick to lead the league in single-season disqualifications?

Q43 Who were Ossie Schechtman, Stan Stutz, Jake Weber, Ralph Kaplowitz, and Leo Gottlieb?

Q44 New York's home opener took place on November 11, 1946, at the Garden. The Knicks and Chicago Stags participated in the first overtime match. Who scored New York's first points in their 78–68 loss?

Q45 Who was the shortest player to see action for the Knicks in a regular-season game?

Q46 Who was the first Knick to crack the 40-point barrier in an NBA game?

Q47 The Knicks signed the first black player to an NBA contract in 1950. Who was he?

Q48 Which Knick won the NCAA Outstanding Player Award for two consecutive seasons—1960 and 1961?

Q49 Name the Knick pivotman who was guarding Wilt Chamberlain when the Big Dipper notched 100 points on March 2, 1962.

Q50 In his career, he played with nine different NBA teams, the most of any Knick. Who was this center?

Q51 Bill Bradley set an NCAA playoff scoring record for a single game in 1965 when he registered 58 points for Princeton. Who was the opponent in that game?

Q52 Name the three teams for whom Dick Barnett played in his 15-year NBA career.

Q53 With what major league team did Dave DeBusschere play baseball?

Q54 What two Knicks were back-to-back NIT MVPs in the 1967 and 1968 tournaments?

Q55 Upon his retirement, what Knick became the doorkeeper of the Georgia Senate?

NEW YORK KNICKS

A42   Ken Bannister (1984–85: 16 games)

A43   The Knicks' first starting lineup (1946–47)

A44   Ossie Schechtman

A45   Wat Misaka (1947–48; 5′7″)

A46   Carl Braun (December 6, 1947: 47 points vs. Providence Steamrollers)

A47   Nat (Sweetwater) Clifton (from the Harlem Globetrotters)

A48   Ohio State's Jerry Lucas

A49   Darrall Imhoff

A50   Len Chappell (the teams are, in order, Syracuse, Philadelphia, New York, Chicago, Cincinnati, Detroit, Milwaukee, Atlanta, Cleveland)

A51   Wichita State

A52   Syracuse, the Lakers, and Knicks

A53   Chicago White Sox

A54   1967: Walt Frazier (Southern Illinois); 1968: Don May (Dayton)

A55   Walt Bellamy

THE UNIFORMS

Q56   Henry Bibby's brother also played professional sports. How did John Bibby distinguish himself in pro baseball?

Q57   Who combined to form the "Rolls-Royce Backcourt"?

Q58   Bill Bradley's NCAA Division I tournament record of 58 points in a single game (1965) was surpassed in 1970. Who broke Dollar Bill's mark?

Q59   Jerry Lucas set an NCAA Division I tournament record when he pulled down 30 rebounds in a game against Kentucky in 1961. Who surpassed his performance just two years later?

Q60   In which category is Walt Frazier NOT the Knicks' all-time career leader?

        (a) Field goal attempts   (c) Free throw attempts
        (b) Field goals made   (d) Free throws made

Q61   With what team did Walt Frazier end his career in 1980?

Q62   Who were the Knicks' original "Twin Towers"?

Q63   Who led the NBA in three-point field goal percentage in the 1981/82 season?

Q64   Who preceded Patrick Ewing as the starting center for New York in the 1984/85 season?

Q65   Bernard King scored 50 points in consecutive games during the 1983–84 season. Before King, who was the last NBA player to do this?

Q66   Mark Jackson set a league rookie mark with 868 assists in 1987. Whose NBA record did he break?

Q67   Kiki Vandeweghe's uncle was once a Knick. Name this player from the 1957/58 season.

Q68   Why did Trent Tucker choose to wear No. 6?

Q69   Name the two players who set a Knick standard by sinking 36 consecutive free throws.

NEW YORK KNICKS

A56 He pitched the first no-hitter for the Texas Rangers in August 1973

A57 Walt Frazier and Earl Monroe

A58 Notre Dame's Austin Carr (61 points vs. Ohio)

A59 Bowling Green's Nate Thurmond (1963: 31 rebounds vs. Mississippi State)

A60 (d)—the club high is held by Richie Guerin

A61 Cleveland Cavaliers

A62 Bill Cartwright (7′1′′) and Marvin Webster (7′0′′)

A63 Campy Russell (.439)

A64 Pat Cummings

A65 Rick Barry (1966–67)

A66 Oscar Robertson's record

A67 Mel Hutchins

A68 He selected the number because he was the sixth overall player taken in the 1982 draft

A69 Kiki Vandeweghe and Henry Bibby

Q1. Who is the founding father of the New York Knicks?

Q64. Who preceded Patrick Ewing (above) as the starting center for New York in the l984-85 season?

Q82. This man succeeded Willis Reed as the Knicks' starting center in the 1974–75 season. Name him.

Q111. This former Knick established the NBA's "iron man" record by playing in 906 consecutive games. Who is he?

Q70 What is Trent Tucker's given first name?

Q71 Patrick Ewing was voted onto the 1990 starting Eastern Conference All-Star team. Before Ewing, who was the last Knick to be a starting All-Star?

Q72 Match the Knick with his nickname.

(1) Dick Barnett   (a) Sweetwater
(2) Nat Clifton   (b) Popeye
(3) Dennis Layton   (c) Fall Back Baby
(4) Forest Weber   (d) Mo
(5) Whitey Bell   (e) Jake

—REED—

Q73 Willis Reed was the second-round choice of the Knicks in the 1964 draft. Name the 6′8″ Texas cager taken in the first round.

Q74 Name the high school rival Willis Reed edged out for NBA Rookie of the Year honors in 1964.

Q75 In 1965 and 1966, Willis Reed played in the All-Star Game and set an NBA record in the process. What was unique about Reed's back-to-back appearances?

Q76 Willis Reed played forward for the better part of four seasons (1965–66 through 1968–69). Who were the starting centers during that time?

Q77 Who backed up Reed during the 1969/70 championship season?

Q78 Willis Reed is the only basketball player to achieve the "triple play of honors" in 1970. What three awards did he win?

Q79 In a gritty display of courage, Willis Reed played virtually on one leg in the seventh game of the 1970 championship series against the Lakers. The Knick captain tore a muscle, but refused to give up, and his play earned him the MVP award. How many points did Reed score?

Q80 For how many consecutive seasons was the Captain named to the All-Star team?

NEW YORK KNICKS

A70   Kelvin

A71   Bob McAdoo (1977)

A72   1—c; 2—a; 3—d; 4—e; 5—b

A73   Jim "Bad News" Barnes

A74   Luke Jackson (Philadelphia)

A75   He was named as the All-Star center in 1965 and was honored as a forward the following year, the first man in league history to achieve that feat

A76   1965–66: Len Chappell; 1966–67 and 1968–69: Walt Bellamy

A77   Nate Bowman

A78   Regular-season MVP, playoff MVP, and All-Star MVP

A79   Four

A80   Seven (Reed first became an All-Star in his rookie season, 1964–65, and was last named in the 1970–71 season; he never made the team after that)

THE UNIFORMS

Q81 What two players vied for the center position after Willis Reed called it quits?

Q82 Who succeeded Reed as the Knicks' starting center in the 1974–75 season?

GLORY DAYS

Q83 Name the Knick who has played in the most postseason games.

Q84 Only four Knicks have registered more than 40 points in a single playoff game. Who are they?

Q85 What Knick tied Bob Cousy's NBA playoff record of 51 assists in a four-game series?

Q86 Who is the only man in NBA history to play for a club during the postseason, but not play a game with that team during the regular season?

Q87 New York made the playoffs in their first season. The Knicks lost their first postseason game, but won the series. Whom did they play?

Q88 New York made it to the finals for the first time in 1951. To whom did they lose in seven games?

Q89 With the score tied at 75 in the seventh game of the 1951 championship series, Rochester's Bob Davies was fouled with 40 seconds left. Davies sank both free throws to win the game and the NBA crown. Who committed the foul?

Q90 Name the starting lineup of the 1969–70 champion Knicks.

Q91 Name the only Knick who played in the final round of an NBA championship series prior to the 1970 playoffs.

Q92 What two teams did New York defeat on their way to the 1969–70 championship series?

NEW YORK KNICKS

A81 John Gianelli and Neal Walk

A82 John Gianelli

-------------------------- · --------------------------

A83 Bill Bradley—95 games in eight seasons (Walt Frazier leads in postseason minutes played, with 3,953 in 93 games)

A84 Bernard King, Patrick Ewing, Willis Reed, and Bob McAdoo

A85 Walt Frazier (1969: against Baltimore)

A86 Jerry Fleishman (1953—by special permission, he was picked up by New York for the playoffs after several Knicks were sidelined because of injuries; during the regular season, Fleishman played for the Philadelphia Warriors)

A87 Cleveland Rebels (April 2, 1947: Rebels 77, Knicks 51; New York won the series, 2–1)

A88 Rochester Royals

A89 Dick Maguire

A90 Guards: Walt Frazier and Dick Barnett; forwards: Bill Bradley and Dave DeBusschere; center: Willis Reed

A91 Dick Barnett (with the 1962 Lakers)

A92 Eastern Division semifinals: Baltimore Bullets (4–3); Eastern Division finals: Milwaukee Bucks (4–1)

Q93 How many consecutive games did the Knicks win in their championship year of 1969–70?

Q94 Game 3 of the 1970 championship series would have been lost if the three-point shot had been in effect. What Laker sank a 60-foot shot in the last seconds of regulation to throw the game into overtime?

Q95 Willis Reed was the Knicks' high scorer in the 1970 playoffs. Who ranked second in scoring?

Q96 Name the seven members of the 1972–73 championship team who are enshrined in basketball's Hall of Fame.

Q97 What two members of the 1973 championship team did not play on the Knicks' 1969–70 team?

Q98 What two teams did New York defeat on their way to the 1973 championship series?

Q99 When the Knicks won the world championship in 1973, they finished second in the Atlantic Division. Who was first?

Q100 New York won the 1973 NBA championship in a 4–1 series victory over L.A. What Hall of Famer played his last game in the series?

Q101 Who was the Knicks' leading scorer in the 1973 playoffs?

Q102 What five members of the 1973 championship series (the Knicks and Lakers) have been head coaches in pro basketball?

Q103 Who was the last member of the 1973 championship team to play for the Knicks?

Q104 What Knick scored the most playoff points in a two-game series?

Q105 Trent Tucker's four-point play, the first in Knick history, almost saved the day in Game 6 of the 1988–89 Eastern Conference semifinals against Chicago. Who fouled Tucker on the play?

NEW YORK KNICKS

A93   18 (it was a league record at the time)

A94   Jerry West (New York won in OT, 111–108)

A95   Dick Barnett

A96   Willis Reed, Jerry Lucas, Walt Frazier, Earl Monroe, Bill Bradley, Dave DeBusschere, and head coach Red Holzman

A97   Jerry Lucas and Earl Monroe

A98   Eastern Conference semifinals: Baltimore Bullets (4–1); Eastern Conference finals: Boston Celtics (4–3)

A99   Boston Celtics

A100   Wilt Chamberlain (in his last game, Wilt played all 48 minutes, scored 23 points, and had 21 rebounds in the 102–93 fifth-game loss to the Knicks)

A101   Walt Frazier (373 points, 21.9 per game)

A102   New York: Willis Reed (Knicks), Dave DeBusschere (Detroit); L.A.: Jerry West (Lakers), Wilt Chamberlain (San Diego Conquistadors), Pat Riley (Lakers)

A103   Earl Monroe (1979–80 season)

A104   Bob McAdoo (1978: 68 points vs. Cleveland)

A105   Craig Hodges

Q106 The Knicks ended a long string of losses at the Boston Garden when they defeated the Celtics in the fifth and decisive game of the 1990 playoffs. How many had they lost prior to the April victory?

Q107 Who is the all-time Knick leader in average points per game (minimum three seasons)?

Q108 The quickest disqualification of a Knick from a game occurred within nine minutes of the opening tip-off. Who was the player involved?

Q109 Who set the single-game club record by blocking 10 shots?

Q110 Patrick Ewing shares the record of playing in 18 NCAA Division I tournament games. With what former Knick does he share this mark?

Q111 What former Knick established the NBA's iron man record by playing in 906 consecutive games?

Q112 The 1950–51 Knicks still hold the NBA record for playing in the most overtime games in a season. In how many extra-period contests did they participate?

Q113 The Knicks set a league record when they won 18 consecutive games during the 1969/70 season. What two teams shared the old record of 17 straight victories?

Q114 Who was the first Knick to lead the league in scoring for the season?

Q115 Which team did the Knicks hold to 19 field goals—the lowest total since the introduction of the shot clock?

Q116 Harry Gallatin holds the team record for playing in 610 consecutive games. Who is a distant second with 361 games?

Q117 What Knick holds the dubious distinction of being disqualified the most times in one year?

NEW YORK KNICKS

A106 26 games

A107 Bob McAdoo (26.7 ppg)

A108 Paul Noel (November 20, 1949: against Philadelphia)

A109 Joe C. Meriweather (December 12, 1979: against Atlanta)

A110 Bill Martin (Martin, who played eight games with New York in the 1986–87 season, was a four-year teammate of Patrick Ewing's at Georgetown)

A111 Randy Smith

A112 13 overtime games

A113 Washington (1946–47) and Boston (1959–60)

A114 Bernard King (1984–85: 32.9 ppg)

A115 Indiana Pacers (December 12, 1985: New York won, 82–64)

A116 Ray Felix (1954–59)

A117 Ken Bannister (he was ejected 16 times during the 1984–85 season)

SETTING THE STANDARD

Q118   Dick McGuire set a team rookie record with 386 assists in the 1949 season. Who is the only first-year Knick to surpass him?

Q119   Who set a team record when he hit 19 consecutive field goals?

Q120   This Knick impressed his new teammates as he grabbed 343 offensive rebounds in 1988–89, setting a new club record. Name this chairman of the boards.

Q121   Who holds the season record for three-pointers?

TRADES, WAIVES, AND ACQUISITIONS

Q122   New York has had the first overall pick in the NBA draft four times. Whom did they select with those choices?

Q123   What four St. John's University players were selected in the first round of the draft by the Knicks?

Q124   Who was the first player taken by the Knicks in the NBA's first draft (1947)?

Q125   Although they were both rookies in 1964, Em Bryant was four years older than Willis Reed when the Mutt and Jeff combo joined the team. Bryant did not go directly to college when he finished high school. What did he do for four years, and from what school was he ultimately drafted?

Q126   Name the 1965 first-round draft pick of the Knicks who missed two seasons (1967–68 and 1968–69) because of a heart attack.

Q127   Name the 1963 first-round draft choice of the Cincinnati Royals who was selected while he was in high school.

Q128   From what team was Dave DeBusschere obtained on December 19, 1968?

Q129   Whom did New York give up for the services of Dave DeBusschere?

NEW YORK KNICKS

A118 Mark Jackson (1987–88: 868 assists; Jackson's total also surpasses Oscar Robertson's NBA rookie mark of 690)

A119 Johnny Newman (January 1–8, 1988)

A120 Charles Oakley

A121 Trent Tucker (1988–89: 118 three-pointers on 296 attempts; he broke his own record of 69 the previous season)

A122 Art Heyman (1963), Jim Barnes (1964), Cazzie Russell (1966), and Patrick Ewing (1985)

A123 Dick McGuire (1949), Johnny Warren (1969), Mel Davis (1973), and Mark Jackson (1987)

A124 Utah's Wat Misaka

A125 Bryant joined the Air Force, and after his duty was over, he enrolled in a junior college. A year later he went to DePaul on a basketball scholarship.

A126 Dave Stallworth (Stallworth returned in 1969 and played six more seasons in the NBA, including four with New York)

A127 Jerry Lucas (Lucas sat out his first year so he could attend Ohio State University)

A128 Detroit Pistons (at the time, he was the player/coach)

A129 Walt Bellamy and Howie Komives

TRADES, WAIVES, AND ACQUISITIONS

Q130 Prior to the 1971–72 season, the Knicks sent Cazzie Russell to San Francisco. Whom did they receive in return?

Q131 Earl Monroe was acquired by the Knicks in 1971 from the Baltimore Bullets. Name the two players traded for the Pearl.

Q132 Charles Oakley came to New York in a trade with Chicago. Who went to the Windy City in the deal?

Q133 What team picked Ernest "Kiki" Vandeweghe in the first round of the 1980 NBA draft?

NEW YORK KNICKS

A130 Jerry Lucas

A131 Dave Stallworth and Mike Riordan

A132 Bill Cartwright

A133 Dallas (he never came to terms with the Mavericks and was traded to Denver, where he played for four seasons)

*** FAST FACTS ***

Knicks Coaching Records (as of the 1989–90 season)

	Regular Season			Playoffs		
	Won	Lost	Pct.	Won	Lost	Pct.
Ned Cohalan (1946/47)	33	27	.550	2	3	.400
Joe Lapchick (1947/48–1955/56)	326	247	.569	30	30	.500
Vince Boryla (1955/56–1957/58)	80	85	.485	0	1	.000
Fuzzy Levane (1958/59–1959/60)	48	51	.485	0	2	.000
Carl Braun (1959/60–1960/61)	40	87	.315	0	0	.000
Eddie Donovan (1961/62–1964/65)	84	194	.302	0	0	.000
Harry Gallatin (1964/65–1965/66)	25	38	.397	0	0	.000
Dick McGuire (1965/66–1967/68)	75	102	.424	1	3	.250
Red Holzman (1967/68–1976/77; 1978/79–1981/82)	613	484	.559	54	43	.557
Willis Reed (1977/78–1978/79)	49	47	.510	2	4	.333
Hubie Brown (1982/83–1986/87)	142	202	.413	8	10	.444
Bob Hill (1986/87)	20	46	.303	0	0	.000
Rick Pitino (1987/88–1988/89)	90	74	.549	6	7	.462
Stu Jackson (1989/90)	52	35	.549	4	6	.400
Total	1677	1719	.494	107	109	.495

New Jersey Nets

NEW JERSEY NETS

1975–76 ABA Champions

Front row (left to right): Chuck Terry, Tim Bassett, Jim Eakins, Julius Erving, Kim Hughes, Rich Jones, trainer Fritz Massmann
Back row (left to right): Owner Roy Boe, John Williamson, Ted McClain, assistant coach Bill Melchionni, coach Kevin Loughery, Brian Taylor, George Bucci, Al Skinner

THE SUITS

Q1 How many coaches have led the Nets since their inception in 1967?

Q2 What two Net coaches did Bob MacKinnon succeed in midseason?

Q3 Who was the Nets' first head coach?

Q4 Who was the Nets' second head coach and the first to take them into postseason play?

Q5 What was unique about Lou Carnesecca's coaching contract?

Q6 How long was Carnesecca at the Nets' helm?

Q7 Kevin Loughery coached the Nets from the 1973–74 season, gained two ABA championships, and saw the admittance of the organization into the NBA before retiring in mid-1980–81 with a 12–23 record. Who replaced Loughery behind the bench that year?

Q8 Head coach Larry Brown resigned with six games remaining in the 1982–83 season to take the same position with a college team. To what school did he go?

Q9 At what school was Willis Reed head coach?

Q10 Prior to his tenure with New Jersey, what NBA team had Bill Fitch coached?

NEW JERSEY NETS

A1   12 coaches

A2   Kevin Loughery (1981) and Dave Wohl (1987)

A3   Max Zaslofsky (1967–68 and 1968–69)

A4   York Larese (one season: 1969–70; record: 39–45)

A5   He signed the contract prior to the 1969–70 season, but did not start as head coach until the following season so he could fulfill his obligation to his employer, St. John's University

A6   Three seasons (1970–71 through 1972–73)

A7   Assistant coach Bob MacKinnon (MacKinnon left coaching with a 12–35 record and became the new general manager at the end of the season)

A8   University of Kansas (he was replaced for the last six games by assistant coach Bill Blair)

A9   Creighton University (Reed was also assistant coach under Lou Carnesecca at St. John's for one year)

A10   Cleveland (nine seasons), Boston (four seasons), and Houston (five seasons)

Q11   Under what three names have the Nets played?

Q12   The Nets have had five home courts since their inception in 1967. Name them.

Q13   The Nets and another team petitioned for admission into the NBA in 1975, but were rejected. Name the other franchise.

Q14   In 1976, the ABA and the NBA merged. In addition to the Nets, what three NBA teams participated in the merger?

Q15   What opposing player set an NBA record for turnovers in a game against the Nets?

THE UNIFORMS

Q16   What Net was the second-best three-point shooter in the ABA's first season?

Q17   What player set an ABA record for consecutive free throws made during the 1968 season?

Q18   This All-American from Rutgers was the 1967 NCAA foul-shooting champion. In the 1968–69 season, he set a Net and ABA record by sinking 60 consecutive free throws. Name him.

Q19   What Net is the only player in NCAA history to record over 200 assists and 100 steals in back-to-back seasons?

Q20   Swen Nater led all of pro basketball in the 1974–75 season with 16.4 rebounds per game. Whose three-year ABA reign did he end?

Q21   What Net was the first player to win three NBA titles for most steals in a season?

NEW JERSEY NETS

———————————— · ————————————

A11 New Jersey Americans (1967), New York Nets (1968–77), and New Jersey Nets (1978–present)

A12 Teaneck Armory (Teaneck, N.J.), Commack Arena (Commack, N.Y.), Nassau Veterans Memorial Coliseum (Uniondale, L.I., N.Y.), Rutgers Athletic Center (Piscataway, N.J.), Brendan Byrne Arena (East Rutherford, N.J.)

A13 Denver Nuggets

A14 Indiana Pacers, Denver Nuggets, and San Antonio Spurs

A15 Atlanta's John Drew (March 1, 1978: 14 turnovers)

———————————— · ————————————

A16 Ron Perry (Pittsburgh Piper Chico Vaughn led the league that year)

A17 Bobby Floyd (49 free throws over a 13-game span)

A18 Bob Lloyd

A19 Mookie Blaylock (Oklahoma)

A20 Artis Gilmore's

A21 Michael Ray Richardson

Q22 Darryl Dawkins led the league twice in disqualifications (1982–83 and 1983–84). Who is the only other Net to lead the NBA in the same category?

Q23 Mike Gminski was the second player to have his number retired at his alma mater, Duke. Who was the first?

Q24 Kelvin Ransey's rookie season with Portland was impressive, as he averaged 15.2 points and 6.9 assists per game in 1980. To whom did he lose Rookie of the Year honors by a single vote?

Q25 This player's claim to fame was his role in USC's victory over UCLA in 1968. Thanks to him scoring two baskets—the Trojans' tying and winning points—Lew Alcindor's UCLA Bruins went down to their only defeat of the year. Name the Net who sank the crucial buckets.

Q26 What two Nets were teammates at Vincennes Junior College and combined to win the National Junior College Championship in 1970?

Q27 In the 1985–86 season, Ray Williams registered an NBA first: he spent time with teams from all four divisions. Name the teams.

Q28 What former Net is a cousin of Willis Reed?

Q29 What two Nets never attended college?

Q30 Who was the Nets' 1972 first-round pick from Marquette?

Q31 Bernard King was the Nets' first-round pick in the 1977 draft. For what school did King play?

Q32 Only one Net from the team's first year made the club in the 1969–70 season. Who was he?

Q33 The 1972–73 season marked the first time a Net was chosen as ABA Rookie of the Year. Who was so honored?

Q34 Who was New Jersey's backup center behind Billy Paultz in 1974–75?

Q35 Name the Net whose life was cut short in a 1975 plane crash near New York.

NEW JERSEY NETS

A22 George Johnson (1977–78)

A23 Dick Groat

A24 Darrell Griffith

A25 Ron Taylor

A26 Bob McAdoo and Foots Walker

A27 Atlantic: Nets; Central: Atlanta Hawks; Midwest: San Antonio Spurs; Pacific: L.A. Clippers

A28 Orlando Woolridge (1986–87 and 1987–88)

A29 Darryl Dawkins and Bill Willoughby

A30 Jim Chones

A31 Tennessee (he signed with the team after his junior year)

A32 Walt Simm

A33 Brian Taylor

A34 Willie (Rainbow) Sojourner

A35 Wendell Ladner

Q3. Who was the Nets' first head coach?

Q36. For what team did Rick Barry play before he jumped to the ABA?

Q50. Much to the fans' dismay, Dr. J was sold to the 76ers in 1976. What reason did Nets owner Roy Boe give for the sale?

Q73. In a four-for-one deal, Billy Paultz was traded to San Antonio in 1975. Who came to New Jersey in the transaction?

Q36 For what team did Rick Barry play before he jumped to the ABA?

Q37 Name the guard who teamed with Rick Barry in the Net backcourt and led the ABA in assists for the 1970–71 season.

Q38 Rick Barry played two seasons with the Nets (1970–71 and 1971–72). From what franchise was he obtained?

Q39 Who replaced Rick Barry for the first two months of the 1970–71 season when he was out with a foot injury?

—THE DOCTOR—

Q40 In what category did Julius Erving lead the nation while a junior in college?

    (a) Scoring   (c) Assists
    (b) Rebounding   (d) Free-throw percentage

Q41 How many ABA scoring titles did Julius Erving win?

Q42 At what college did Erving play?

Q43 Which NBA team selected Dr. J in the 1973 collegiate draft?

Q44 Erving approached the Nets before he went to the Virginia Squires, but the club would not sign him. Why did New Jersey reject him?

Q45 While playing for Virginia in the 1972–73 season, Dr. J became head coach for a game. Whom did he replace for a single night?

Q46 How did the Nets acquire Julius Erving in 1973?

Q47 In order to sign Dr. J in 1973, the Nets had to compensate two teams. What clubs were indemnified in the deal?

Q48 With what player did Erving share the 1974–75 ABA MVP award?

Q49 Dr. J fell short of the 1974–75 ABA scoring title by a mere 20 points. Who nosed him out for the honor that season?

Q50 Much to the dismay of the fans, Erving was sold to the 76ers in 1976. What reason did Nets owner Roy Boe give for the sale?

NEW JERSEY NETS

A36 San Francisco Warriors (1965–66 and 1966–67)

A37 Bill Melchionni

A38 Virginia Squires

A39 Ollie Taylor

A40 (b)

A41 Three (1972–73, 1973–74, and 1975–76)

A42 University of Massachusetts

A43 Milwaukee Bucks

A44 The organization had a policy prohibiting the signing of undergraduates (Erving left school after his junior year)

A45 Al Bianchi (Before Bianchi left to scout the Squires' opponent in the upcoming playoffs, he made Erving coach for a game against the Nets. In the last game of the season, Dr. J coached Virginia to a 123–117 win.)

A46 The Virginia Squires sent Erving and Willie Sojourner to the Nets for George Carter, the draft rights to Kermit Washington, and cash

A47 The Virginia Squires (for whom Erving was playing) and the Atlanta Hawks (who had purchased and held his NBA rights)

A48 Indiana Pacer George McGinnis

A49 Indiana's George McGinnis (2,343 points to 2,363)

A50 He needed the $3 million to cover the NBA entry fee

THE UNIFORMS

Q51 Julius Erving won three ABA scoring titles (1971–72, 1973–74, and 1975–76). How many times did he lead the NBA in scoring?

GLORY DAYS

Q52 Only two teams won more than one ABA championship. The Nets were one. Name the other club.

Q53 The Nets made the playoffs for the first time in 1971. Whom did they meet in the Eastern Semifinals?

Q54 After a strong showing the previous year, Nets fans were disappointed when the team lost in the first round of the 1973 playoffs. Who upset them in the Eastern Division semifinals?

Q55 In their fifth consecutive postseason appearance, the Nets won the ABA championship. Whom did they defeat for the 1974 title?

Q56 What playoff record did the Nets establish on their way to the 1974 ABA championship?

Q57 In the 1974–75 season, the Nets tied for first place in their division but lost a one-game playoff to determine the winner. Who defeated them?

Q58 Favored to repeat as ABA champions, the 1974–75 Nets fell in the opening round. Who ousted them from the playoffs in five games?

Q59 Whom did the Nets defeat to win their second (and the league's last) ABA championship?

Q60 What team was the Nets' first postseason opponent after the NBA and ABA merged?

Q61 In 1984 the Nets registered their first series win in NBA postseason play. Whom did they defeat?

NEW JERSEY NETS

A51 None

_____ · _____

A52 Indiana Pacers (the Pacers won three crowns, while the Nets won two)

A53 Virginia Squires (Squires won the series, 4–2)

A54 Carolina Cougars (4–1)

A55 Utah Stars (4–1)

A56 Fewest losses (in three series and 14 games, they lost only two games)

A57 Kentucky Colonels

A58 Spirits of St. Louis

A59 Denver Nuggets (4–2; the Nuggets were heavily favored)

A60 Philadelphia 76ers (1979: 76ers won in two games)

A61 Philadelphia 76ers (they eliminated Philadelphia 3–2 in the series before bowing to Milwaukee in the Eastern Conference semifinals, 4–2)

_____ · _____

SETTING THE STANDARD

Q62   Who set an NBA record for assists in one game with 29?

Q63   Darryl Dawkins is one of three players to lead the league in fouls in three seasons. Name the other two.

Q64   Michael Ray Richardson set an NBA record when he led the league for three seasons (1979–80, 1982–83, 1984–85) in steals. For what three teams did Richardson play when he established the mark?

Q65   Whose record did Kevin Porter surpass when he dished out 29 assists in a game against Houston during the 1977–78 seasons?

Q66   The Nets set an NBA futility record by losing 34 consecutive road games. What team did they defeat to end the streak?

Q67   Whose record for consecutive road losses did the Nets surpass?

TRADES, WAIVES, AND ACQUISITIONS

Q68   Name the two brothers who were both first-round selections of the Nets.

Q69   What was the first trade ever made by the Nets?

Q70   Who was the first draft selection of the Nets in their premiere season, 1967?

Q71   True or false: The Nets drafted Lew Alcindor in the same year (1969) that Milwaukee selected the superstar.

Q72   The Nets pulled a coup in 1970 when two top prospects were signed by the franchise. Who were the coveted frontliners?

NEW JERSEY NETS

A62   Kevin Porter (February 24, 1978; against Houston)

A63   Minneapolis's George Mikan and Vern Mikkelsen

A64   Knicks (1979–80), Golden State Warriors/Nets (1982–83), and Nets (1984–85)

A65   San Francisco's Guy Rogers's (March 14, 1963: 28 assists)

A66   Phoenix Suns (November 23, 1990: 116–114)

A67   Baltimore Bullets (1957–58: 33 games)

_____ . _____

A68   Bernard King (1977–79) and Albert King (1981)

A69   Net Jim Caldwell went to Kentucky for Stewart Johnson

A70   Sonny Dove, St. John's University

A71   True (Milwaukee offered more money, and Alcindor opted for the Bucks)

A72   Billy Paultz and Jim Ard

*** FAST FACTS ***

Nets Seasonal Leaders

Total points—Rick Barry, 1971–72: 2,518
Average—Rick Barry, 1970–71: 29.4
Rebounds—Buck Williams, 1981–82: 1,105
Steals (since 1976–77)—Michael Ray Richardson, 1984–85: 243

TRADES, WAIVES, AND ACQUISITIONS

Q73 In a four-for-one deal, Billy Paultz was traded to San Antonio in 1975. Who came to New Jersey in the transaction?

Q74 Before coming to the Nets in the dispersal draft (1976), Jan van Breda Kolff played with two ABA teams. Name them.

Q75 Name the player who was traded to Indiana in 1977 for a first-round draft choice and was reacquired by the Nets in 1978 from the Pacers for Bob Carrington and two second-round draft choices.

Q76 To what team and for whom did New Jersey trade Brian Taylor and two first-round picks in 1976?

Q77 Who came to New Jersey when the Nets sent Al Skinner to the Detroit Pistons?

Q78 Otis Birdsong was the Houston Rockets' 1977 first-round draft pick and the second player selected overall. Who was chosen ahead of Birdsong?

Q79 Who was the Nets' first draft choice after they merged with the NBA?

Q80 Halfway through the 1979–80 season, the Nets acquired Maurice Lucas and two first-round draft choices from Portland. Name the player who was sent to the Trail Blazers.

Q81 While playing for New Orleans, Rich Kelley distinguished himself as an able rebounder. What three players were sent to the Jazz for the rights to Kelley?

Q82 Who were the Nets' two first-round selections in the 1980 draft?

Q83 In 1981, Otis Birdsong ranked second on Houston's all-time scoring roster (behind Elvin Hayes). Whom did the Nets give up to acquire Birdsong?

Q84 On August 17, 1982, New Jersey obtained Darryl Dawkins from the 76ers. Whom did they send to Philadelphia for Double D?

Q85 Whom did New Jersey acquire when they dispatched Eric Floyd and Mickey Johnson to Golden State in 1983?

NEW JERSEY NETS

A73 Kim Hughes, Swen Nater, Rich Jones, and Chuck Terry

A74 Denver Nuggets (1974–75) and Virginia/Kentucky Squires (1975–76)

A75 John Williamson

A76 Kansas City; Nate Archibald

A77 Kevin Porter and Howard Porter

A78 Milwaukee chose Kent Nelson

A79 Forward Bernard King (1977)

A80 Calvin Natt (he was the Nets' 1979 first-round pick from Northeast Louisiana)

A81 Bernard King, John Gianelli, and Jim Boylan

A82 Mike O'Koren (North Carolina) and Mike Gminski (Duke) (they were selected with the draft choices obtained from Portland in the Calvin Natt/Maurice Lucas trade)

A83 Cliff Robinson (Robinson never played for the Rockets, but was traded shortly after to Kansas City)

A84 A number one draft choice (1983) and cash

A85 Micheal Ray Richardson

TRADES, WAIVES, AND ACQUISITIONS

Q86 Fred Roberts was involved in a unique trade in 1983. The New Jersey Nets had to give Roberts to San Antonio as compensation for this player. Name him.

Q87 In order to select Tate George in the first round of the 1990 draft, the Nets had to swap players with Chicago. Whom did New Jersey give up in the deal?

Q88 Seattle gave New Jersey the draft rights to Jud Buechler for not taking this player in the 1990 draft. Name him.

Q89 When the Nets traded Buck Williams to Portland, they received Sam Bowie and the Blazers' first pick in the 1990 draft. Whom did they select with the choice?

NEW JERSEY NETS

A86   Head coach Stan Albeck (when the Spurs' coach bolted to New
Jersey, San Antonio demanded the services of Roberts)

A87   Dennis Hopson

A88   Dennis Scott

A89   Oklahoma's Mookie Blaylock

*** FAST FACTS ***

Nets Coaching Records (as of the 1989–90 season)

	Regular Season			Playoffs		
	Won	Lost	Pct.	Won	Loss	Pct.
Max Zaslofsky (1967/68–1968/69)	53	103	.359	0	0	.000
York Larese (1969/70)	39	45	.462	3	4	.429
Lou Carnesecca (1970/71–1972/73)	114	138	.452	13	17	.433
Kevin Loughery (1973/74–1980/81)	297	318	.483	21	13	.618
Bob MacKinnon (1980/81)	12	35	.255	0	0	.000
Larry Brown (1981/82–1982/83)	91	67	.576	0	0	.000
Bill Blair (1982/83)	2	4	.333	0	2	.000
Stan Albeck (1983/84–1984/85)	87	77	.530	5	9	.357
Dave Wohl (1985/86–1987/88)	65	114	.363	0	3	.000
Bob MacKinnon (1987/88)	10	29	.256	0	0	.000
Willis Reed (1987/88–1988/89)	33	77	.300	0	0	.000
Bill Fitch (1989/90)	17	65	.207	0	0	.000
Total	803	1007	.444	42	48	.467

New York Rangers

NEW YORK RANGERS

1939–40 Stanley Cup Champion New York Rangers

THE SUITS

Q1 Who was the millionaire sportsman responsible for the formation of the Rangers in 1926?

Q2 Conn Smythe was the Ranger's first GM, but he was fired before the season began for refusing to sign a player. Who was that player?

Q3 Who was the team's second general manager and first coach?

Q4 What was Lester Patrick's nickname?

Q5 Name the Ranger coach who appeared in the Stanley Cup playoffs in every one of his 16 playing years.

Q6 What Ranger coach introduced these practices: the box defense, aggressive penalty killing, and removing the goalie in favor of a sixth skater?

Q7 Name the two brothers who coached the Rangers (at different times) in the late 1940s and 1950s.

Q8 The Broadway Blueshirts kept the family tradition alive when they hired this former Ranger to succeed Muzz Patrick behind the New York bench in 1955. Who was he?

Q9 What was Emile Francis's nickname?

Q10 For what teams and at what position did Emile Francis play in his pro career?

Q11 When did Emile Francis take charge of the Blueshirts?

Q12 What was Francis's first act as GM of the Rangers?

Q13 General manager Emile Francis took drastic measures over what he considered an apathetic attitude by his Ranger squad. What did the Cat do to his entire roster during the 1975–76 campaign?

Q14 How many separate tenures did Emile Francis have as coach of the Rangers?

Q15 Whom did Boom Boom Geoffrion replace behind the Ranger bench in 1968?

NEW YORK RANGERS

A1   Tex Rickard

A2   Babe Dye (he was never signed by the Rangers)

A3   Lester Patrick

A4   "The Silver Fox"

A5   Bernie "Boom Boom" Geoffrion (Montreal and the Rangers)

A6   Frank Boucher

A7   Lynn Patrick (1948–50) and Muzz Patrick (1954–55 and three months in 1962)

A8   Phil Watson

A9   "The Cat"

A10   The Chicago Black Hawks (1946–47) and the Rangers (1948–49); goalie

A11   October 30, 1964 (prior to becoming GM and coach, he led Guelph of the OHA and was Assistant GM of the Rangers)

A12   He fired the Rangers coach, Red Sullivan, and took over the position himself

A13   Francis put the whole team on waivers

A14   Three (1965–68, 1969–73, 1974–75)

A15   Emile Francis

Q16 Name the coach who benched Rod Gilbert, the league's top right winger, for a game in 1974 because the player was late for a team meeting.

Q17 What school did Herb Brooks lead to three NCAA championships in 1974, 1976, and 1979?

Q18 After spending several years in Philadelphia, Fred Shero became the Rangers' coach and general manager in 1978. In what unorthodox way did the Rangers acquire Shero?

Q19 In 1980, Michel Bergeron was given the assistant coaching position with the Quebec Nordiques, but within two weeks he was promoted to head coach. Whom did he replace at the helm?

Q20 With what five clubs had Roger Neilson held the head coaching position before coming to New York?

Q21 GM Neil Smith never skated in the NHL, but played two seasons in the International Hockey League. What NHL organization drafted Smith?

Q22 With whom did Neilson share coaching duties behind the Black Hawk bench?

F.Y.I.

Q23 Against what club have the Rangers won the most games?

Q24 Who faced off against the Rangers in their opening game on Garden ice, November 16, 1926?

Q25 Which team has defeated New York the most times?

Q26 Against what team have the Rangers netted the most goals?

Q27 Name the only two players who have had their numbers retired by the Rangers.

NEW YORK RANGERS

A16 Larry Popein (Popein was fired shortly after the incident; he coached the team from June 1973 to January 1974)

A17 University of Minnesota

A18 Shero came to New York in exchange for the team's first draft choice and cash

A19 Maurice Filion

A20 Toronto (1977–78 and 1978–79), Buffalo (1979–80 and 1980–81), Vancouver (1981–82 through 1983–84), Los Angeles (1983–84), and Chicago (1984–85 through 1986–87)

A21 New York Islanders (1974)

A22 Bob Pulford (in Chicago)

_____ . _____

A23 Chicago Black Hawks (223 wins in 547 games played—as of 1990)

A24 Montreal Maroons (Rangers won, 1–0, on a Bill Cook goal)

A25 Montreal (283 losses in 526 games—as of 1990)

A26 Boston Bruins (1,590 goals in 547 games—as of 1990)

A27 Eddie Giacomin (No. 1) and Rod Gilbert (No. 7)

Q28 In the club's first season, the Rangers beat out four U.S. cities to win the American Division of the NHL. Name the other teams in New York's division.

Q29 Distressed by their poor showing in the early 1950s, the Rangers brought a professional in to boost the team's confidence. Whom did they hire?

Q30 New York finished first in their division in the 1989–90 season. How many years was it since they last accomplished that feat?

Q31 For the first time in team history, New York swept the season series from this team in 1989–90. Whom did they defeat?

Q32 The Rangers registered their 1,000th home-ice win on January 14, 1990. Who was their opponent?

THE UNIFORMS

Q33 Two goalies are credited with playing 70 games in a season. Who were they?

Q34 Name the former Ranger who holds the all-time record for shutouts.

Q35 On two separate occasions, a Ranger goalie was credited with two assists in one game. Name those scoring machines.

Q36 Who holds the club record for career shutouts?

Q37 Name the New York netminder who accrued 56 minutes in penalties in one season.

Q38 Who was the starting goalie for the Rangers in the 1928 Stanley Cup finals?

Q39 What 44-year-old hockey legend stepped in as the disaster goalie in the 1928 Cup finals against Montreal and allowed just one score?

NEW YORK RANGERS

A28 Boston Bruins, Chicago Black Hawks, Pittsburgh Pirates, and Detroit Red Wings

A29 A hypnotist (he was fired after one game because the team lost)

A30 48 years (the last time was in the 1941–42 season)

A31 Boston Bruins (the Rangers won all three games)

A32 Philadelphia Flyers (4–3)

A33 Eddie Giacomin (1968–69 and 1969–70) and Johnny Bower (Bower played in every game of the 1953–54 season)

A34 Terry Sawchuk (1949–50 through 1969–70: 103 shutouts)

A35 Eddie Giacomin (March 19, 1972: against Toronto) and John Vanbiesbrouck (January 9, 1985: at Winnipeg)

A36 Ed Giacomin (50 shutouts, including 49 in the regular season)

A37 Bob Froese (1986–87)

A38 Lorne Chabot

A39 Lester Patrick (the Rangers prevailed, 2–1, and took the Cup)

Q40 In the game mentioned above, name the injured netminder Patrick replaced.

Q41 The NHL extended the area in front of the net after this Ranger goalie complained that the crease was not wide or deep enough. Who was he?

Q42 At the end of the 1951–52 season, the Rangers, mired in fifth place, sent goalie Emile Francis to the AHL. The Cat's replacement gave up 17 goals in three games and never played in another NHL contest. Who was he?

Q43 Name the 1960 Olympic star who was the first American born goaltender to play for the Rangers.

Q44 This goalkeeper played two seasons with the Rangers (1963–64 and 1964–65) and is credited with popularizing the use of face masks. Who was this innovative net minder?

Q45 Who was traded to Montreal for Jacques Plante before the start of the 1964 season?

Q46 Name the two goalkeeps who brought the Vezina (NHL's best goaltender) Trophy to New York in 1971.

Q47 Name the Ranger goalie whose mask depicted a jungle cat, an animal the player believed he was a reincarnated version of.

Q48 Name the Ranger netminder who was the first goalie to jump directly from junior hockey to the NHL (St. Louis Blues).

Q49 What Ranger netminder debuted with a 2–1 win over the Colorado Rockies while he was still with his junior club, Sault Ste. Marie?

Q50 What three players are ahead of Phil Esposito in the all-time point leader category?

Q51 This iron man played in 630 consecutive games with the Rangers and Bruins from 1955 through 1964. Who was he?

Q52 Who scored the Rangers' first penalty shot?

Q53 Name the last Ranger to lead the league in penalty minutes.

NEW YORK RANGERS

A40 Lorne Chabot

A41 Chuck Rayner

A42 Lorne Anderson

A43 Jack McCartan

A44 Jacques Plante

A45 Gump Worsley

A46 Eddie Giacomin and Gilles Villemure

A47 Gilles Gratton (1976–77)

A48 John Davidson

A49 John Vanbiesbrouck (December 5, 1981)

A50 Wayne Gretzky, Gordie Howe, and Marcel Dionne

A51 Andy Hebenton

A52 Bert Connolly (January 24, 1935: against Toronto's George Hainsworth)

A53 Reg Fleming (1941–42: 166 minutes—he split his time between Boston and New York)

Q54 Who was the Rangers' first Rookie of the Year winner?

Q55 A seven-time winner of the Lady Byng (sportsmanship) Trophy, this player was the first Ranger to draw a major penalty (for fighting). Who was he?

Q56 Who was the first player elected to the Hockey Hall of Fame in the same year that he retired?

Q57 Who won the Frank Boucher Trophy as the Rangers' most valuable player in 1957, 1958, 1959, and 1962?

Q58 Who was the last Ranger to win the Ross Trophy (for the league's highest scorer)?

Q59 What Ranger captain captured both the Hart (NHL MVP) and Lady Byng (sportsmanship) trophies at the close of the 1948–49 season?

Q60 This Ranger was the recipient of the Calder (rookie-of-the-year) and Lady Byng (sportsmanship) trophies in 1954 when he scored 32 goals while accumulating a mere two minutes in penalties. Who was he?

Q61 What league award did Andy Bathgate win in 1958–59, when he had 89 points?

Q62 Wayne Gretzky won an unprecedented seven consecutive Ross Trophies (league's leading scorer) from 1980/81-1986/87. Who won the award in the season before Gretzky began his streak?

Q63 Who was known as "Lazy Lightning"?

Q64 What is Brad Park's given name?

Q65 Match the early-day Ranger with his real first name.

(a)	Bunny Cook	(1)	Don
(b)	Ching Johnson	(2)	Ivan
(c)	Taffy Abel	(3)	Fred
(d)	Muzz Patrick	(4)	Clarence
(e)	Bones Raleigh	(5)	Murray

Q66 Who comprised the Rangers' GAG Line, and what did the acronym mean?

NEW YORK RANGERS

A54   Kilby McDonald (1939–40)

A55   Frank Boucher (November 16, 1926)

A56   Dit Clapper (Clapper was actually elected on the same day that he announced his retirement; he called it quits in the afternoon, and the selection committee happened to be meeting that evening)

A57   Andy Bathgate

A58   Bryan Hextall (1941–42)

A59   Buddy O'Connor

A60   Camille Henry

A61   Hart Trophy (league MVP)

A62   Marcel Dionne

A63   Doug Harvey (1961–62 through 1963–64: he never appeared to be working hard)

A64   Douglas

A65   a—3; b—2; c—4; d—5, e—1.

A66   The line consisted of Jean Ratelle, Vic Hadfield, and Rod Gilbert. GAG stood for "goal a game."

THE UNIFORMS

Q67 Who comprised the Rangers' Bulldog Line of 1969–70?

Q68 What Ranger was a harness racing jockey in the off-season?

Q69 Name the Ranger who had a cameo role on *Ryan's Hope*.

Q70 What Ranger was a shortstop on Yale's baseball team behind the Mets' Ron Darling?

Q71 As a member of the NHL rules committee, this Ranger Hall of Famer was credited with the introduction of the red line. Who was he?

Q72 Who was the first Ranger to wear No. 13?

Q73 Who was the Rangers' first team captain?

Q74 Name the Ranger who was the youngest man to play for the team (age 18) and the youngest captain in club history (age 22).

Q75 What Ranger was the first Greek to play in the NHL?

Q76 The Rangers can boast of having had the first European player to skate in the NHL. Name the Swedish import who saw action in the 1964–65 season.

Q77 In the 1930s, Ranger center Frank Boucher pioneered a shot that has become an integral part of the game. What did Boucher develop?

Q78 For 11 years, Ching Johnson was a stalwart on defense for New York. His association with the game did not end when he retired in 1937. What did the Bald Eagle do when his playing days were over?

Q79 This lightning quick center played briefly for the Rangers after 11 years in a Montreal uniform. He was dubbed the Babe Ruth of Hockey, and 50,000 people filed by his casket in the center of the Montreal Forum. Who was he?

Q80 Two brothers and another winger comprised the famed Broad Line in the late 1930s. Name the trio.

Q81 Why was Ranger Billy Taylor expelled from the game for life on March 9, 1947?

NEW YORK RANGERS

A67   Dave Balon, Walt Tkaczuk, and Billy Fairbairn

A68   Gilles Villemure

A69   Ron Greschner

A70   Bob Brooke

A71   Frank Boucher

A72   Jack Stoddard (1951–53)

A73   Bill Cook (1926–27 through 1936–37)

A74   Dave Maloney (1974–75 and 1978–79 respectively)

A75   Ants Atanas (1944–45)

A76   Ulf Sterner (many players resented Sterner's presence in the NHL and subjected him to a great deal of rough treatment; he continued his career in Sweden)

A77   The slap shot

A78   He was an NHL linesman

A79   Howie Morenz (1935)

A80   Neil and Mac Colville, Alex Shibicky

A81   Taylor was charged with associating with gamblers (the suspension was not lifted until 1970)

THE UNIFORMS

Q82 Only one player from the 1960 U.S. Gold Medal team played with New York. Name him.

Q83 He helped create the NHL Players Association in 1957 while a member of the Canadiens' squad. Montreal unloaded him to the Rangers for blue liner Louie Fontinato in 1961. Who was he?

Q84 This player was once hit with 33 penalty minutes in a game against St. Louis in 1974, setting the club's single-game record. Name the Ranger, who played in New York from 1974–75 through 1978–79.

Q85 In 1974, Rod Gilbert was benched for a game because he was late for a team meeting. Who filled his slot on the GAG Line?

Q86 This player became the first native New Yorker to play for the Rangers when he signed as a free agent in the summer of 1976. Name this fan favorite.

Q87 What Ranger winger was credited with scoring the NHL's 100,000th regular-season goal on October 12, 1980?

Q88 Name the four Rangers who played on the USA's Olympic Gold Medal Team of 1980.

Q89 Name the New York native who was selected by Winnipeg in 1980 and became the first Big Apple player drafted directly from a local team.

Q90 What pair of 1980s defensemen were known as the Twin Towers?

Q91 As a teenager, this Ranger worked as a stick boy for the team, and his father was on the Garden maintenance crew. Name the player.

Q92 Who was the only Ranger to score a hat trick in the 1987–88 campaign?

Q93 How many goals did Guy Lafleur register in his lone season with New York?

Q94 In 1961–62, Andy Bathgate was tied for most points in a season, but another hockey superstar was awarded the Ross Trophy on the basis of most goals scored. Who edged out Bathgate?

NEW YORK RANGERS

A82   Jack McCartan

A83   Doug Harvey

A84   Greg Polis

A85   Bobby Rousseau

A86   Nick Fotiu

A87   Wilf Paiement

A88   Bill Baker, Rob McClanahan, Mark Pavelich, and Dave Silk

A89   Brian Mullen

A90   Willie Huber (6′5″) and Barry Beck (6′3″)

A91   Brian Mullen

A92   Ulf Dahlen

A93   18 goals (and 27 assists)

A94   Bobby Hull

Q4. What was Lester Patrick's nickname?

Q5. Name the Ranger coach who appeared in the Stanley Cup playoffs in every one of his 16 playing years.

Q57. This Ranger won the Frank Boucher Trophy as the team's most valuable player in 1957, 1958, 1959, and 1962. Name him.

NEW YORK RANGERS

Q99 Name the three clubs that Phil Esposito played with in his NHL career.

Q95   After "Handy Andy" retired from the NHL in 1971, he suited up for a short time to help a struggling WHA club. For what team did he play?

Q96   The price for Barry Beck was steep, as the Rangers sent five players to the Colorado Rockies on November 2, 1979. Who did the Blueshirts give up in the deal?

Q97   Who drafted Barry Beck with the second overall pick in the 1977 amateur draft?

Q98   Beck was second in the balloting for the 1978 Calder Trophy (Rookie of the Year). Who was first?

—ESPO—

Q99   Name the three clubs that Phil Esposito played with in his NHL career.

Q100   Who was the goalie when Esposito registered the 500th of his 710 career goals?

Q101   Phil Esposito was called a "garbage collector" early in his playing career because he scored many of his goals from rebounds. Off whose shots was he accused of getting his goals?

Q102   What season did Phil Esposito put his name in the record books by becoming the first player in NHL history to score 100-plus points?

Q103   What three uniform numbers did Esposito wear in his six seasons in New York?

Q104   The 72 regular-season goals that Espo netted in the 1970–71 season were another record breaker. Whose scoring mark did he shatter?

Q105   Esposito won the Art Ross Trophy for four consecutive seasons (1970–71 through 1973–74). Who ended his string as the league's highest scorer?

—MARCEL—

Q106   What team originally selected Marcel Dionne with the second overall pick in the 1971 amateur draft?

NEW YORK RANGERS

A95 Vancouver Blazers

A96 Pat Hickey, Lucien DeBlois, Mike McEwen, Dean Turner, and Bobby Crawford

A97 Colorado Rockies

A98 Islander Mike Bossy

A99 Chicago Black Hawks, Boston Bruins, and the Rangers

A100 Detroit's Jim Rutherford (December 22, 1974)

A101 Chicago's Bobby Hull's

A102 1968–69 (he finished with 126 points on 49 goals and 77 assists)

A103 Nos. 5, 12, and 77

A104 Bobby Hull's (58 goals)

A105 Bobby Orr

A106 Detroit Red Wings

*** FAST FACTS ***

Ranger Seasonal Club Records

Most Points: 109 (1970–71 and 1971–72)
Most Wins: 49 (1970–71)
Most Losses: 44 (1984–85)
Most goals: 319 (1974–75)

Q107 What player was chosen ahead of Dionne with the first overall pick in the 1971 draft?

Q108 Marcel Dionne's 500th goal came while he was still with the L.A. Kings. Name the netminder who gave up the milestone score.

Q109 How and when did the Rangers acquire Marcel Dionne?

Q110 True or false: As of 1990, Marcel Dionne is the all-time leader in goals scored by a center.

GLORY DAYS

Q111 The Rangers played in 18 postseason matches in the 1979 playoffs—the most in team history. How many of those contests did they win?

Q112 Six Rangers have registered hat tricks in the Stanley Cup playoffs. Has any Ranger ever scored four (or more) goals in a postseason match?

Q113 In an overtime game against the Atlanta Flames during the 1980 playoffs, a Ranger scored 33 seconds into the extra period. Who netted the fastest OT postseason goal in club history?

Q114 What Ranger had the last hat trick in the postseason?

Q115 Who was the only Ranger awarded a penalty shot in the playoffs?

Q116 Who is the top career scorer for the Rangers in the playoffs?

Q117 Who is the all-time leading playoff scorer (goals and total points) for the Rangers?

Q118 Who holds the Ranger record for shutouts in the playoffs?

Q119 Name the Ranger who is the career leader in penalty minutes in postseason play.

Q120 Name the goalie who registered the last shutout in a playoff game for the Rangers.

NEW YORK RANGERS

A107   Montreal's Guy Lafleur

A108   Washington's Al Jensen

A109   The Rangers traded Tom Laidlaw and Bobby Carpenter to the Kings for Dionne in 1987

A110   True—he has 731 goals at his position

A111   11 (also a club record)

A112   No

A113   Steve Vickers (April 8, 1980)

A114   Ron Duguay (April 20, 1980: against Philadelphia's Pete Peeters; Rangers won the quarterfinal game, 4–2)

A115   Anders Hedberg (April 17, 1981: he scored against St. Louis' Mike Liut)

A116   Rod Gilbert (67 points; he is also the top goal scorer, with 34 in 79 playoff games)

A117   Rod Gilbert (79 games, 34 goals, 67 points)

A118   Dave Kerr (seven times)

A119   Ching Johnson (1926–27 through 1936–37: 159 minutes)

A120   John Vanbiesbrouck (April 8, 1987: division semifinals at Philadelphia; 3–0)

*** FAST FACTS ***

Ranger Seasonal Player Records

Most Goals: Vic Hadfield, 50 (1971–72)
Most Assists: Mike Rogers, 65 (1981–82)
Most Points: Jean Ratelle, 109, 46 goals and 63 assists (1971–72)
Most PIM: Troy Mallette, 305 minutes (1989–90)
Most Shutouts: John Ross Roach, 13 (1928–29)

Q121 The Rangers have the dubious distinction of being the first established NHL team to be eliminated in the playoffs by an expansion club. What upstart team bumped off the Rangers?

Q122 The fastest overtime goal scored against the Rangers in the playoffs took place in 1975 in the preliminary round. Who scored at 11 seconds into the extra period?

Q123 How many times have the Rangers met the Islanders in the playoffs?

Q124 New York made the playoffs in the first year of their existence (1926–27), but lost in the first round. Who knocked them out of action?

Q125 The Rangers won their first Stanley Cup in 1928. What club did they defeat in the finals that year?

Q126 Who scored the overtime goal in Game 5 of the 1928 finals that won the game and brought the Cup to New York?

Q127 In the 1939 semifinal series against Boston, this Bruin scored the winning overtime goal in three of the seven games played. Who was the Rangers' nemesis?

Q128 What team and what goalie did Pete Stemkowski beat when he lit the red lamp in the third overtime of the 1971 Stanley Cup semis?

Q129 The last time New York made it to the Cup finals was in 1979 against the Canadiens. What was the result?

Q130 Who led the Rangers in the 1990 playoffs with seven goals and 12 points?

Q131 The tone of the 1990 playoffs against the Islanders was set in Game 1 when Pat LaFontaine was flattened and had to be hospitalized. Name the Ranger who sent LaFontaine sprawling.

Q132 What team ended the Rangers' 1989–90 season in the Patrick finals?

Q133 The Rangers' 1990 Stanley Cup hopes were dashed when they lost the division finals four games to one, with the last two ending in overtime. Name the goal scorers who defeated New York in the extra periods.

NEW YORK RANGERS

A121 Philadelphia Flyers (1974 semifinals)

A122 Islander J. P. Parise

A123 Six times (their record is 2–4)

A124 Boston Bruins (after the first game ended in a 0–0 tie, the Rangers lost the second match and were eliminated from the playoffs)

A125 Montreal Maroons

A126 Frank Boucher

A127 Mel Hill (Boston won the series, 4–3, and the Cup)

A128 Tony Esposito was in goal for the Chicago Black Hawks

A129 Montreal won, 4–1

A130 Bernie Nicholls

A131 James Patrick (the Rangers won the Patrick semis, 4–1)

A132 Washington Capitals (4 games to 1)

A133 Game 3: Rod Langway (0:34 of overtime); Game 4: John Druce (6:48 of overtime)

Q134 Who holds the team record for both seasons and games played in a Ranger uniform?

Q135 Name the Ranger who is tied for second on the all-time league list for seasons played.

Q136 The 1943–44 Rangers had the worst start in NHL history. How many consecutive games did they drop from opening day?

Q137 Who surpassed Andy Hebenton's iron man league record of 630 consecutive games?

Q138 The 1954–55 Ranger record for home ties has been equaled four times, but never broken. What is the mark?

Q139 Who scored 50 goals in one season—the most by any Ranger?

Q140 What Ranger equaled an NHL rookie record by potting five goals in one game?

Q141 Brian Leetch's 23 goals is a league record for rookie defensemen. Whose NHL mark did he surpass?

Q142 Name the Ranger who set a club record by scoring a goal in 10 consecutive games.

Q143 Name the only two Rangers to net five goals in a game.

Q144 Rod Gilbert holds the team record for 20-goal seasons (12), but who is the club leader in 30-goal seasons?

Q145 A free agent signed by the Rangers in 1983, this center was the first player in league history to score 50 goals with two different teams— Pittsburgh and Montreal. Who was he?

NEW YORK RANGERS

A134   Harry Howell (1952–53 through 1968–69: 17 seasons, 1,160 games)

A135   Tim Horton (24 seasons; he is tied with Alex Delvecchio and is behind Gordie Howe's 26 seasons)

A136   11 games

A137   Garry Unger (914 games; February 24, 1968 through December 21, 1979)

A138   13 ties (while New York set its record in a 70-game season, the others played in either a 76- or 78-game year)

A139   Vic Hadfield (1971–72)

A140   Don Murdoch (October 12, 1976: at Minnesota)

A141   Barry Beck's (1977–78: 22 goals while playing for Colorado)

A142   Andy Bathgate (December 12, 1962 through January 5, 1963)

A143   Don Murdoch (October 12, 1976: against Minnesota) and Mark Pavelich (February 13, 1983: against Hartford)

A144   Jean Ratelle (six years)

A145   Pierre Larouche

SETTING THE STANDARD

Q146 Who potted the fastest three goals in Ranger history against Washington's Mike Palmateer on February 21, 1988?

Q147 With whom is Rod Gilbert tied for the most 20-assist seasons with the Rangers?

Q148 Who established single-season club records during 1971–72 for points (109) and assists (63)?

Q149 Who holds the team record for career penalty minutes?

Q150 Name the player who once registered seven points in one game—the most ever by a Ranger.

Q151 Who established the team's single-season mark with 305 penalty minutes?

Q152 Name the Ranger who set an All-Star record in 1953 for the fastest two goals from the start of the game.

Q153 This Ranger put his name in the record books when he scored 20-plus goals while playing all three forward positions in one season. Name him.

Q154 Which club rookie record did Tony Granato NOT set?

(a) Most goals in a season (36)
(b) Most points in a season (76)
(c) Most shorthanded goals (4)
(d) Most hat tricks (3)

TRADES, WAIVES, AND ACQUISITIONS

Q155 In a player-for-player swap, whom did the Rangers acquire when they dispatched veteran Dean Prentice to the Bruins in 1963?

Q156 Name the five players who came to the Rangers in 1964 after Hall of Famer Andy Bathgate and Don McKenney were shipped to Toronto.

Q157 Whom did Emile Francis unload to sign winger Ron Stewart?

NEW YORK RANGERS

A146 Don Maloney (the goals came within a span of 2:20)

A147 Walt Tkaczuk (both have 13 seasons with 20-plus assist seasons)

A148 Jean Ratelle

A149 Ron Greschner (as of the end of the 1989–90 season, he had 1,226 minutes in penalties)

A150 Steve Vickers (February 18, 1976: three goals and four assists vs. Washington)

A151 Troy Mallette (1989–90)

A152 Wally Hergesheimer (who scored twice within 5:25; the NHL All-Stars beat the Stanley Cup champion Montreal Canadiens)

A153 Pat Hickey

A154 (b)—Mark Pavelich set this record in 1981–82 (76 points)

A155 Don McKenney

A156 Dick Duff, Bob Nevin, Arnie Brown, Bill Collins, and Rod Seiling

A157 Red Berenson (1967)

TRADES, WAIVES, AND ACQUISITIONS

Q158   In March 1970, the Rangers traded Guy Trottier and Denis Dupere to Toronto for a defenseman who founded a doughnut chain that bears his name. Who was this veteran player?

Q159   Who was the Rangers' first selection in the 1973 Universal Amateur Draft?

Q160   The Rangers acquired Derek Sanderson from Boston in 1974. Whom did they send to Beantown for the Turk?

Q161   Following the 1974 season, Emile Francis broke up the GAG Line by trading Vic Hadfield to the Pittsburgh Penguins. Who came to New York?

Q162   The Bruins shocked the hockey world when they traded their star center, Phil Esposito, to the Rangers. Who else was involved in the blockbuster deal?

Q163   Whom did former Ranger GM John Ferguson select instead of Mike Bossy in the first round of the 1977 draft?

Q164   Name the two brothers who played at Providence College and were both selected by the Rangers in the 1980 draft.

Q165   Marcel Dionne became a Ranger on March 10, 1987. What King also came east in the transaction?

Q166   What did the acquisition of Bernie Nicholls cost the Rangers?

Q167   As compensation for signing Guy Lafleur, Quebec gave New York their fifth-round pick in the 1980 draft. Whom did the Rangers select with the choice?

NEW YORK RANGERS

A158 Tim Horton

A159 Rick Middleton

A160 Walt McKechnie

A161 Nick Beverley

A162 Espo and Carol Vadnais came to New York for Brad Park, Jean Ratelle, and Joe Zanussi

A163 Ron Duguay

A164 Scot and Kurt Kleinendorst (Kurt never played for New York)

A165 Jeff Crossman (along with a 1989 third-round draft pick)

A166 Tomas Sandstrom and Tony Granato

A167 Sergei Zubov

*** FAST FACTS ***

Ranger First-Round Draft Picks, 1976 through 1990
[( ) indicates overall choice]

1976:	Don Murdoch (6)
1977:	Lucien DeBlois (8)
1978:	Don Maloney (26)
1979:	Doug Sulliman (13)
1980:	Jim Malone (14)
1981:	James Patrick (9)
1982:	Chris Kontos (15)
1983:	Dave Gagner (12)
1984:	Terry Carkner (14)
1985:	Ulf Dahlen (7)
1986:	Brian Leetch (9)
1987:	Jayson More (10)
1988:	Troy Mallette (22)
1989:	Steven Rice (20)
1990:	Michael Stewart (13)

New York Islanders

NEW YORK ISLANDERS

1983 Stanley Cup Champion
New York Islanders

Q1 Whom did Roy Boe appoint as the Isles' first GM?

Q2 Name the four men who have coached the Islanders.

Q3 What is Al Arbour's real first name?

Q4 Name the four teams for whom Al Arbour played.

Q5 What team did Arbour coach prior to the New York Islanders?

Q6 Who is the only man in the NHL to coach in more games than Al Arbour?

Q7 Coach Terry Simpson once sent three players to the showers because he was frustrated with the team's lackluster performance. It occurred in a 1987 game with Toronto when New York registered only 11 shots-on-goal in the first two periods. Name the three skaters.

Q8 Who is the only man to coach more games with one team than Al Arbour?

F.Y.I.

Q9 Whom did New York meet in their first regular-season game?

Q10 Who scored the winning goal in that game?

Q11 Who scored the first goal against New York?

Q12 The club's first victory came on October 12, 1972. Whom did the Isles defeat?

Q13 It was only 10 days into their inaugural season before the Islanders were shut out for the first time in their history. What goalie whitewashed the Isles?

NEW YORK ISLANDERS

A1   Bill Torrey

A2   1972–73: Phil Goyette and Earl Ingarfield; 1973–74 through 1985–86, 1989–90 to present: Al Arbour; 1986–87 through 1989: Terry Simpson

A3   Alger

A4   Detroit Red Wings, Chicago Black Hawks, Toronto Maple Leafs, and St. Louis Blues

A5   St. Louis Blues (he coached them for 50 games during the 1970 season before resuming his playing career)

A6   Dick Irvin (1930–31 through 1955–56: 1,437 games)

A7   Gerald Diduck, Mikko Makela, and Brad Lauer

A8   No one (Arbour broke Billy Reay's record of coaching one team)

A9   Atlanta Flames (October 7, 1972: Atlanta won, 3–2)

A10   Atlanta's Rey Comeau

A11   Flame Morris Stefaniw (at 12:48 of the first period)

A12   L.A. Kings (3–2)

A13   Pittsburgh's Denis Herron (October 17, 1972)

Q14 The Isles were one of two teams to enter the NHL in 1972. Name the other.

THE UNIFORMS

Q15 Who were the Islanders' first two goaltenders?

Q16 Chico Resch was second in the voting for the 1976 Calder Trophy (Rookie of the Year). Who was the winner?

Q17 To what team was Chico Resch traded during the 1980–81 season?

Q18 The Islander netminders won the 1983 William Jennings (team goaltending) Trophy with a 2.83 GAPG. Who led the team in regular-season games played (44), goals against (2.66), and games won (24)?

Q19 In Billy Smith's rookie year, he played in only five games with the L.A. Kings. Name the two goalies he played behind on the West Coast.

Q20 What league record did Billy Smith break in his first season with the Islanders?

Q21 Billy Smith was the first goalie in NHL history to tally a goal. What team surrendered the historic score?

Q22 In 1980 and again in 1982, Billy Smith set an NHL playoff mark by winning 15 postseason games in one year. Who broke his record?

Q23 Billy Smith finished second in saves percentage among all 1983–84 goaltenders (.896). Who was first?

Q24 Between 1983 and 1985, Billy Smith started in 33 consecutive playoff games. Who ended his streak in Game 2 of the 1985 Patrick Division semifinals?

Q25 Denis Potvin was named captain of the Isles in the 1979–80 season and retained the honor through the club's four Stanley Cup victories. Whom did he replace in that role?

NEW YORK ISLANDERS

A14 Atlanta Flames

A15 Gerry Desjardins was drafted from Chicago and Billy Smith was taken from L.A. in the 1972 expansion draft

A16 Bryan Trottier

A17 Colorado Rockies (he went to the Rockies with Steve Tambellini for Mike McEwen and loan rights to Jari Kaarela)

A18 Rollie Melanson

A19 Rogatien (Rogie) Vachon and Denis DeJordy

A20 Most penalty minutes (42) by a goaltender

A21 Colorado Rockies (1979)

A22 Edmonton's Grant Fuhr (1988: 16 games)

A23 Teammate Rollie Melanson

A24 Kelly Hrudey

A25 Clark Gillies

Q26   Name the two Islander 50-goal scorers.

Q27   Who registered the club's first goal?

Q28   Who assisted on New York's first goal?

Q29   Who scored the Islanders' first shorthanded goal?

Q30   Who scored the Isles' first power-play goal?

Q31   Who registered the club's first hat trick?

Q32   Name the players who combined for the club's fastest two goals.

Q33   Who registered the club's 100th goal in December 1973 against the Montreal Canadiens?

Q34   The Islanders' first successful penalty shot came on February 1, 1975, in a road game. Name the skater who lit the red lamp.

Q35   Name the Islander who set an AHL record by scoring 11 shorthanded goals in a season.

Q36   Name the player who led the team in both goals and total points in the Isles' first year.

Q37   The first penalty called on an Islander was for boarding at 17:42 of the first period in the club's inaugural game. Who committed it?

Q38   The first major penalty assessed against an Islander was for fighting. The battle was with their crosstown rivals, the Rangers. Who was charged with the penalty?

Q39   In 1976, two Islanders were honored by the NHL. Name the players who snared the Calder Trophy (best rookie) and the Norris Trophy (best defenseman) that year.

Q40   Who was the first player in the NHL to sweep the Lady Byng (sportsmanship) and Bill Masterton (dedication) trophies in one year (1978)?

Q41   Who was the first Islander to receive the Hart Trophy as the league's Most Valuable Player?

NEW YORK ISLANDERS

A26 Mike Bossy and Pat LaFontaine

A27 Ed Westfall (October 7, 1972: against Atlanta; at 17:29 of the second period)

A28 Germain Gagnon (against California's Marv Edwards)

A29 Ed Westfall (October 7, 1972: against Atlanta; at 19:29 of the second period)

A30 Germain Gagnon (November 1, 1972: against California Seal Gilles Meloche)

A31 Clark Gillies (4:51) and Mike Bossy (4:57) (October 27, 1979: six seconds against Chicago)

A32 Gerry Hart (against goalie Wayne Thomas)

A33 Lorne Henning (against Detroit's Jim Rutherford)

A34 Gary McAdam

A35 Germain Gagnon and Dave Hudson

A36 Bill Harris (28 goals, 50 points)

A37 Ken Murray

A38 Billy Smith (October 21, 1972: at 0:39 of the second period; he was fighting with Rod Gilbert)

A39 Calder: Bryan Trottier; Norris: Denis Potvin

A40 Butch Goring (he was with L.A. at the time)

A41 Bryan Trottier (1979)

Q42 Who was the MVP in the 1979 Challenge Cup versus the Russians?

Q43 Who was the Isles' first team captain?

Q44 Who is the only player to win the Stanley Cup and an Olympic gold medal in the same year?

Q45 Only two Islanders played in all 78 games of the 1972–73 season. Who were they?

Q46 No sooner was this player acquired in a 1973 trade with Atlanta than he was injured and out for the season. Who was this unlucky skater?

Q47 Who was the last Islander from the 1972–73 team to leave the club?

Q48 Bob Bourne almost made his living on the diamond. What major league baseball team was interested in the Islander forward?

Q49 With what club did John Tonelli play prior to arriving in New York in 1978?

Q50 Dave Langevin was drafted by New York in 1974 but did not play with the Islanders until 1979. What caused the delay?

Q51 Butch Goring was given a piece of hockey equipment when he was 12 years old. He used it throughout his 16-year career and it became his trademark. What was Goring's prized possession?

Q52 Duane and Brent Sutter came from a hockey family. Name the six Sutters who played in the NHL.

Q53 The Isles registered only one game-tying goal in the 1988–89 season. Who scored it?

Q54 It was only nine games into the 1988–89 season before Brad Lauer was hit by a slap shot and knocked out for most of the season. Name the Flyer who caused the injury.

NEW YORK ISLANDERS

A42 Clark Gillies

A43 Eddie Westfall

A44 Ken Morrow (1980)

A45 Billy Harris and Brian Spencer

A46 Ernie Hicke (he was hit by Philadelphia's Bill Flett)

A47 Billy Smith (1988–89)

A48 Houston Astros

A49 Houston Aeros of the WHA

A50 He elected to play for Edmonton of the World Hockey Association from 1974 until 1979. In 1979, he was selected by the Islanders in the expansion draft.

A51 A helmet

A52 Brent, Duane, Brian, Darryl, Rich, and Ron

A53 Randy Wood

A54 Mark Howe (October 29, 1988: in Philly)

Q55 Match the Islander with his nickname.

(a) Craig Cameron   (1) Toy Tiger
(b) Duane Sutter   (2) Dog
(c) Gary Howatt   (3) Knuckles
(d) Clark Gillies   (4) Gunner
(e) Bob Nystrom   (5) Jethro

—BOSSY—

Q56 Mike Bossy's 53 goals as a rookie still stand as an NHL record. Whose mark of 44 goals by a first-year player did he surpass?

Q57 How many consecutive seasons did Mike Bossy score more than 50 goals?

Q58 In Bossy's 69-goal season, he had one four-goal game. Against what team did he accomplish the scoring bonanza?

Q59 Bossy tied a playoff record when he netted nine goals in a 1983 series. Whom were the Islanders playing?

Q60 How many hat tricks did Bossy have in the 1983 playoffs?

Q61 Who would equal his postseason record-setting total for hat tricks in the same year?

Q62 Who was in the net when Mike Bossy scored his 500th career goal?

Q63 On what occasion did Bossy register his 500th goal?

Q64 Bossy's 1981–82 147-point total was an NHL record for right wingers and made him the third player to break the 140-point plateau. Who were the first two?

Q65 What trophy did Bossy win in 1983, making him the first Islander to be so honored?

Q66 How many teams passed on Mike Bossy in the 1977 draft because he had a reputation for not checking?

NEW YORK ISLANDERS

A55   a—4; b—2; c—1; d—5; e—3

--- . ---

A56   Buffalo's Richard Martin

A57   Nine (the talented winger notched 38 goals in 1986–87, even though he missed 17 games because of an injured back)

A58   Philadelphia Flyers (in the second-to-last game of the 1978–79 season)

A59   Boston Bruins (New York won the Wales Final, 4–2)

A60   Three

A61   Edmonton's Mark Messier

A62   No one (Bossy shot into an empty net on January 2, 1986, as the Isles defeated Boston, 7–5)

A63   Denis Potvin Night at the Nassau Coliseum

A64   Phil Esposito and Wayne Gretzky

A65   Lady Byng Trophy

A66   14 teams

Q21. Billy Smith was the first goalie in NHL history to tally a goal. What team surrendered the historic score?

NEW YORK ISLANDERS

Q63. On what occasion did Mike Bossy register his 500th goal?

Q67 Which single-year playoff record did Bossy NOT set in 1981?

(a) Most power-play goals (9)
(b) Most game-winning goals (5)
(c) Most goals (19)
(d) Most points (35)

—POTVIN—

Q68 From what junior hockey club was Denis Potvin snatched in the 1973 draft?

Q69 Against what team did Denis Potvin register his first goal on October 2, 1973?

Q70 After winning three Norris Trophies (1976, 1978, and 1979), Potvin fell six votes shy of earning a fourth in 1981. Who edged him out for the honor?

Q71 Bobby Orr's record of 914 total points by a defenseman was broken by Denis Potvin in the 1985–86 season. Who was between the pipes when the Isles star equaled Orr's mark?

Q72 Potvin broke Bobby Orr's record for goals by a defenseman in a 1986 game against the Toronto Maple Leafs. Name the goalie who was beaten on the play.

Q73 Whose record of 683 assists by a defenseman did Potvin break in 1986?

Q74 On whose goal did Denis register his record assist?

GLORY DAYS

Q75 Bob Nystrom's four overtime goals in postseason play is second in the NHL record books. Whose is first?

Q76 What two Islanders are one-two in the NHL record books for career power-play goals in the playoffs?

NEW YORK ISLANDERS

A67 (c)—Flyer Reggie Leach scored 19 goals in the 1976 playoffs; Bossy had 17 in 1981

A68 Ottawa 67s

A69 New York Rangers (Potvin registered his first two goals that night against goalie Ed Giacomin)

A70 Pittsburgh's Randy Carlyle

A71 Quebec's Clint Malarchuk (Potvin scored a goal for his 914th point)

A72 Tim Bernhardt

A73 Brad Park's

A74 Bryan Trottier's score

A75 Montreal's Maurice (the Rocket) Richard's

A76 Mike Bossy (35) and Denis Potvin (27)

Q77   In 1980, this Islander tied a playoff mark by scoring three shorthanded goals in New York's four series. Name this player.

Q78   Who registered eight shorthanded goals in Stanley Cup play?

Q79   Name the four teams that fell to New York in the Stanely Cup finals.

Q80   When the Islanders made their remarkable comeback against the Penguins in the 1975 playoffs, they rallied from a 3–0 deficit to take the series. Who tallied the lone goal in the seventh game?

Q81   This Islander set a Stanley Cup record when he scored a goal at the 0:11 mark of the overtime period in the 1975 playoffs. His score also resulted in the Isles winning the preliminary round over the Rangers. Name this player.

Q82   This Islander's most memorable games came in the playoffs. He scored the game and series winner against Buffalo in 1976 and assisted on Ed Westfall's game-winner in the seventh match against Pittsburgh in 1975. Name him.

Q83   Who set the NHL playoff record of four consecutive game-winning goals during the 1977 postseason?

Q84   In the 1979 semifinal playoff series with the Rangers, two of the games went into overtime. Name the two Islanders who scored the winning goals.

Q85   Before the Islanders went on a tear by winning four Stanley Cups and 19 consecutive playoff rounds, who defeated them in the 1979 semifinals?

Q86   On their way to the 1980 Cup, New York played in seven overtime games. What was their record in those contests?

Q87   Who clinched the victory and the Stanley Cup with an overtime score in Game 6 of the 1979–80 Islanders–Flyers series?

Q88   Name the two Islanders in that contest who assisted on the game-winning overtime goal.

Q89   Only one player from the team's 1972 expansion draft shared in the fruits of the 1980 Stanley Cup. Who was he?

NEW YORK ISLANDERS

A77 Lorne Henning

A78 Ed Westfall (his NHL record was broken by Mark Messier and Wayne Gretzky)

A79 1980: Philadelphia; 1981: Minnesota; 1982: Vancouver; 1983: Edmonton

A80 Ed Westfall (against Penguin goalie Gary Innes)

A81 Jean Paul Parise

A82 Defenseman Al Marshall

A83 Clark Gillies (scored against Chicago and Buffalo)

A84 Game 2: Denis Potvin; Game 4: Bob Nystrom

A85 New York Rangers

A86 6–1 (their only loss came at the hands of the Bruins)

A87 Bob Nystrom (it was the year the Isles captured their first Cup)

A88 John Tonelli and Lorne Henning

A89 Billy Smith

*** FAST FACTS ***

Islander Seasonal Records

Most Points: 118 (1981–82)
Most Wins: 54 (1981–82)
Most Losses: 60 (1972–73)
Most Goals: 385 (1981–82)

Q90 The 1980–81 Isles notched another win on their Stanley Cup belt as Mike Bossy set a postseason mark with 35 points, Bryan Trottier had a point in each playoff game, and Denis Potvin set a record for points by a blueliner. None of these impressive facts qualified them for the Conn Smythe Award (for most valuable player in a playoff game). Which Islander walked off with the trophy?

Q91 Who won the Conn Smythe Trophy for the 1982 playoffs?

Q92 Though this player missed the entire 1982 playoff season with a broken bone in his hand, the club petitioned the league to have his name inscribed on the Stanley Cup. Who was so honored?

Q93 Who won the 1983 Conn Smythe Trophy?

Q94 Who scored the OT goal in Game 5 of the Subway Series between the Isles and Rangers in the 1983–84 semifinals?

Q95 For the first time in six seasons the Islanders did not reach the Stanley Cup finals in 1985. Who ended New York's string with a defeat in the Patrick Division finals?

Q96 In the deciding game of the 1987 Cup playoffs, the Isles and Caps battled to a fourth overtime period until this player notched the deciding goal. Who ended the marathon game and who was in goal for New York and Washington?

Q97 Both matches won by the Isles in the 1988 semifinals loss to the Devils were overtime victories. Name the skaters who netted the winners.

Q98 The Islanders set a new NHL record for consecutive wins (February 20, 1982). How many did they string together?

Q99 The Islanders have twice scored 11 goals in a game. Against what two opponents did they set their club mark?

Q100 The Islanders set an NHL record by losing 60 of 78 games in their opening season. What club surpassed their mark?

Q101 What was significant about the Islanders' point total of 1975–76?

Q102 The 1977–78 Islanders tied a league record by having six 30-or-more-goal scorers on the club. Name the New York sharpshooters.

NEW YORK ISLANDERS

A90 Butch Goring

A91 Mike Bossy

A92 Hector Marini

A93 Billy Smith

A94 Ken Morrow (the Isles won the fifth and final game on his goal)

A95 Philadelphia Flyers (4–1)

A96 Pat LaFontaine knocked in the game-winner at 8:47 of the fourth overtime. Kelly Hrudey was in the nets for the Isles and Bob Mason was guarding the web for Washington.

A97 Game 1: Pat LaFontaine (6:11 of overtime); Game 3: Brent Sutter (15:07 of overtime)

A98 15 wins

A99 Pittsburgh (December 20, 1983) and Toronto (March 3, 1984)

A100 Washington Capitals (1974–75: 67 losses in 80 games)

A101 The Islanders were the youngest team (from the franchise's inception) to rack up more than 100 points in a season (they had 101 points)

A102 Mike Bossy (53), Bryan Trottier (46), Clark Gillies (35), Denis Potvin, Bob Nystrom, and Bob Bourne (30 each)

Q103 What Islander set the club rookie mark by chalking up 95 points in the first season?

Q104 Who is the Isles' single-season point leader at left wing?

Q105 What Isle set an NHL record by scoring six points in a period?

Q106 Name the goalie who set the club record with seven shutouts in one season.

Q107 Who is New York's all-time leader in penalty minutes?

Q108 Name the skater who registered 356 minutes in the penalty box—the most of any Islander in one year.

Q109 Name the Islander who once scored a goal five seconds after the opening face-off, tying an NHL record.

TRADES, WAIVES, AND ACQUISITIONS

Q110 The Islanders have had the first overall selection in the entry draft twice. Whom did they select with those choices?

Q111 The Isles' first amateur choice, Billy Harris, signed a three-year contract with the team. What was unique about the pact?

Q112 The last player taken by the Islanders in their first draft—1972—made the team and proved to be a hardworking winger. Who was he?

Q113 In 1972, the Islanders received Denis DeJordy, Germaine Gagnon, Tony Featherstone, Murray Anderson, and Chico Resch for cash and a second round selection in the 1973 amateur draft. With what team did New York trade?

Q114 It was Potvin & Potvin as the Islanders obtained Denis's older brother Jean from the Flyers. Who was dealt to the City of Brotherly Love in the 1973 deal?

NEW YORK ISLANDERS

A103   Bryan Trottier (1975–76: 95 points)

A104   John Tonelli (1984–85: 100 points on 42 goals and 58 assists)

A105   Bryan Trottier (December 23, 1978: against the Rangers; he had three goals and three assists in the second period on the way to a 9–4 win)

A106   Glenn Resch (1975–76)

A107   Garry Howatt (1,466 minutes)

A108   Brian Curran (1986–87)

A109   Bryan Trottier (March 22, 1984: at Boston)

A110   Billy Harris (1972) and Denis Potvin (1973)

A111   The $100,000-per-year contract was the richest offered to a junior player who had never skated in the NHL

A112   Garry Howatt (taken in the 13th round with the 144th pick overall, Howatt remained with the Isles for nine seasons)

A113   Montreal Canadiens

A114   Terry Crisp

TRADES, WAIVES, AND ACQUISITIONS

Q115 New York acquired Ernie Hicke from the Atlanta Flames in February 1973. Whom did they give up for him?

Q116 The trade that brought Bob Bourne to New York cost the Islanders two players in 1974. Name the skaters who went to the Kansas City Scouts in the deal.

Q117 GM Bill Torrey engineered the 1975 trade that shipped Doug Rombough, Ernie Hicke, and Craig Cameron to Minnesota for two talented forwards. Name the pair that came to New York.

Q118 Jean Potvin was traded during the 1977–78 season and reacquired in the 1979 expansion draft. For what two clubs did he play in between?

Q119 Bill Torrey orchestrated one of the best trades in team history when he sent Billy Harris and Dave Lewis to the Kings for this veteran center. Who came to the Isles?

Q120 Pat LaFontaine was chosen with the third overall pick in the 1983 entry draft. From what club was his draft position acquired?

Q121 On November 25, 1988, New York completed a trade with Chicago that brought Gary Nyland and Marc Bergevin to the Islanders. Who went to the Windy City?

NEW YORK ISLANDERS

A115 Arnie Brown

A116 Bart Crashley and the rights to Larry Hornung

A117 Jude Drouin and J. P. Parise

A118 He was traded to Cleveland in 1978 and drafted from Minnesota in 1979

A119 Butch Goring

A120 Colorado Rockies (the Isles sent Bob Lorimer and Dave Cameron for the pick)

A121 Steve Konroyd and Bob Bassen

*** FAST FACTS ***

Islander Individual Records

Most Seasons: Billy Smith, 17 seasons (1972–73 through 1988–89)
Most Games: Bryan Trottier, 1,123
Most Goals (career): Mike Bossy, 573
Most Points (career): Bryan Trottier, 1,353 (500 goals, 853 assists)
Most Penalty Minutes (career): Garry Howatt, 1,466
Most Shutouts (career): Glenn Resch, 25 (1974–81)
Most Shutouts (one season): Glenn Resch, 7 (1975–76)
Longest Consecutive Games Streak:
  Bill Harris, 576 (October 7, 1972 through November 30, 1979)
Most Goals (season): Mike Bossy, 69 (1978–79)
Most Assists (season): Bryan Trottier, 87 (1978–79)
Most Points (season): Mike Bossy, 147 (1981–82: 64 goals, 83 assists)
Most Points–Rookie (season): Bryan Trottier, 95 (1975–76:
  32 goals, 63 assists)

New Jersey Devils

1984–85 New Jersey Devils

THE SUITS

Q1 Who purchased the Colorado Rockies and moved them to New Jersey?

Q2 Who sold the Rockies franchise?

Q3 Of what other pro sports franchise is Devils chairman John McMullen a majority owner?

Q4 Name the five head coaches who have led the Devils since their 1982 arrival in New Jersey.

Q5 With what team was Billy MacMillan an assistant coach in 1979–80?

Q6 Billy MacMillan became coach of the franchise when the team played in Denver. Whom did he succeed behind the bench?

Q7 MacMillan's coaching career was cut short when he was fired 20 games into the 1983–84 season with a 2–18 start. Who finished the season at the Devils' helm?

Q8 Max McNab, the Devils' one-time GM and vice-president, was a head coach from 1966–71. Name the team McNab led.

Q9 Name the NHL teams Jim Schoenfeld played for in his 13-year career.

Q10 Former skipper Jim Schoenfeld is the official spokesman for a Buffalo-based business. What type of product does Schony advertise?

Q11 For what WHA club did John Cunniff play from 1972–74?

Q12 Before arriving in New Jersey, John Cunniff had a brief stint as an NHL coach during the 1982–83 season. Name the team.

F.Y.I.

Q13 The Devils opened their first season with a 3–3 tie at the Meadowlands. Who was their opponent?

NEW JERSEY DEVILS

A1   Chairman John McMullen (he bought the franchise and transferred it to the Meadowlands as a public service to his native state)

A2   Peter Gilbert

A3   The Houston Astros

A4   Billy McMillan (GM/coach: 1982–83); Tom McVie (1983–84); Doug Carpenter (1984–88); Jim Schoenfeld (1988–89 and 1989–90); John Cunniff (1989–90 to present)

A5   New York Islanders

A6   Don Cherry (Cherry was the Rockies coach for the 1980–81 season)

A7   Tom McVie (his record was 15–38–7)

A8   WHL San Diego Gulls

A9   Buffalo (1973–74 through 1981–82, 1984–85), Detroit (1981–82 through 1982–83), and Boston (1983–84)

A10   Beds

A11   Hartford Whalers

A12   Hartford Whalers (1982–83: 13 games)

A13   Pittsburgh Penguins (October 5, 1982)

Q14 Who netted the first goal against the Devils?

Q15 The team's first win, a 3–2 victory, took place in the Devils' second game. Whom did they defeat?

Q16 It was five games into the 1982–83 season before the Devils lost their first NHL game. What club defeated New Jersey, 5–3, on the Devils' home ice?

Q17 An ex-Rockie was responsible for scoring the first hat trick against the Devils on November 1, 1982. Who was the sniper?

Q18 In what two NHL divisions has the franchise played?

Q19 What were the Blades, Meadowlanders, and Americans?

Q20 In the Devils' first season (1982–83), the team finished with 48 points (17–49–14 record). What two teams had a poorer record?

Q21 The Devils tied a league mark in the 1985–86 season for fewest ties in an 80-game season. What is the record?

Q22 In one of the Devils' most controversial games, a disputed goal by Ranger Robbie Ftorek resulted in a 4–4 tie and an eventual overtime win by New York in January 1985. Name the referee who allowed the disputed goal to stand.

Q23 What is the 334 Club?

Q24 What team did John MacLean's game-winning goal defeat in overtime, allowing the Devils to clinch their first playoff spot in April 1988?

THE UNIFORMS

Q25 What two goalies combined for the Devils' first shutout?

Q26 During the 1988–89 season, Sean Burke set a franchise single-season record for goalies when he was slapped with 54 penalty minutes. Whose team record did he surpass?

NEW JERSEY DEVILS

A14   Pittsburgh's Pat Boutette (October 5, 1982: at 16:18 of the second period)

A15   Rangers (October 8, 1982: 3–2)

A16   Montreal Canadiens (October 14, 1982)

A17   Calgary's Lanny McDonald

A18   Smythe and Patrick (the team played in the Smythe Division when it was the Kansas City Scouts and Colorado Rockies)

A19   The runners-up in fan balloting for New Jersey's nickname.

A20   Hartford and Pittsburgh (both teams had 45 points)

A21   Three ties (the record was equaled by the Calgary Flames the following season)

A22   Bryan Lewis (The Devils argued that the puck hit the crossbar, but Lewis would not relent. Tomas Sandstrom scored the Rangers' winner.)

A23   On January 22, 1987, 334 diehard fans braved a blizzard to watch the Devils beat Calgary, 7–5, at the Meadowlands. (Only 13 New Jersey players arrived by game time, and the contest was delayed almost two hours.)

A24   Chicago (4–3 at Chicago)

A25   Ron Low and Glenn Resch (1983: 6–0 over the Red Wings; Low came out in the second period with an injury and Resch completed the game)

A26   Al Smith's (1980–81: 51 PIM)

Q27   What league award did Chico Resch receive in his first full season with the Devils?

Q28   Name the player who scored his 500th career goal against Devil netminder Chico Resch on December 20, 1983.

Q29   Who assumed the goaltending duties after Chico Resch was dealt to Philadelphia in March 1986?

Q30   With what three teams did Bob Sauve play before joining the Devils?

Q31   In what round was Sean Burke selected in the 1985 draft?

Q32   How many games remained in the season when Sean Burke joined the Devils in 1987?

Q33   Who was the last Colorado Rockie to play with the Devils?

Q34   Who scored the Devils' first goal in regular-season play?

Q35   Who scored the Devils' first hat trick?

Q36   Name the first Devil defenseman and the first rookie to score a hat trick.

Q37   Who tallied New Jersey's first power play goal on October 8, 1982?

Q38   This Devil notched the team's first shorthanded goal four games into the first season. Who scored for New Jersey?

Q39   Who netted the Devils' first game-winner?

Q40   Who is on record for scoring the quickest goal in Devil history?

Q41   It took two years before New Jersey recorded an OT goal. On home ice, the Devils edged Hartford, 6–5, with just six ticks left on the clock. Who scored the milestone goal?

Q42   Name the Devil whose first two NHL goals were both game-winners on the road.

NEW JERSEY DEVILS

A27 Bill Masterton Trophy (for dedication)

A28 Guy LaFleur

A29 Alain Chevrier

A30 Buffalo Sabres, Detroit Red Wings, Chicago Black Hawks

A31 Second round (24th pick overall)

A32 13 games

A33 Aaron Broten

A34 Don Lever (October 15, 1982: 3–3 tie against Pittsburgh)

A35 Steve Tambellini (December 3, 1982: Devils beat the Whalers, 6–5)

A36 Uli Heimer was the first blueliner and rookie to score a hat trick, in a 7–6 defeat by the Pens (October 31, 1984).

A37 Steve Tambellini (at 4:49 of the first period against the Rangers)

A38 Don Lever (October 12, 1982: at 5:33 of the second period vs. Boston)

A39 Merlin Malinowski (October 8, 1982: at 17:06 of the second period vs. the Rangers)

A40 Kirk Muller (who scored eight seconds into a game against St. Louis on December 13, 1989)

A41 Jan Ludvig

A42 Brendan Shanahan (1987–88)

Q43 In late 1984, Rocky Trottier put his name in the club record books when he scored on the club's first penalty shot. Against what netminder did he accomplish this?

Q44 Who was the first Devil to notch four goals in a game?

Q45 The team record for the fastest three goals—42 seconds—was set in a February 1985 game against the Maple Leafs at Toronto. Name the Devils who lit the red light.

Q46 In New Jersey's first game, the first minor and major penalties were called against a Devil at the 8:00 mark of the initial period. Who was penalized?

Q47 Whose team record for career penalty minutes did Ken Daneyko surpass?

Q48 Who was the first Devil to start in an All-Star Game?

Q49 In 1988–89, this Devil was named the first Star of the Game in each of his first two NHL appearances. Who is he?

Q50 He played for his father, Bob, at the University of Wisconsin, was the top scorer on the 1980 Olympic team, and is nicknamed "Magic." Who is he?

Q51 Name the Devil whose rights have been held by all three teams in the New York–New Jersey area.

Q52 Who was between the Devils' pipes when Buffalo Hall of Fame center Gil Perreault scored his 500th goal on March 9, 1986?

Q53 This Devil was the first player taken in the 1975 draft. Who was he?

Q54 Who comprised the Kid Line of the 1982–83 and 1983–84 seasons?

Q55 This Devil was the youngest player ever to skate for the Devils when he hit the ice at 17 years old. Name the player.

Q56 Name the players who comprised the Fossil Line.

NEW JERSEY DEVILS

A43   Edmonton's Andy Moog

A44   Pat Verbeek (February 28, 1988; in an 8–6 win over Minnesota)

A45   Tim Higgins (9:22), Uli Hiemer (9:43), and Phil Russell (10:04)

A46   John Wensink

A47   Pat Verbeek (943 PIM)

A48   Sean Burke (1988–89)

A49   Chris Terreri

A50   Mark Johnson

A51   Roland Melanson (Rollie was an Islander 1980–81 through 1984–85. He was traded to the Rangers by the North Stars, but within a few hours, the goalie was swapped to L.A. He joined Jersey as a free agent in August 1989)

A52   Alain Chevrier

A53   Mel Bridgman (he was selected by the Flyers)

A54   Aaron Broten, Paul Gagne, and Jeff Larmer

A55   Craig Wolanin (1985)

A56   Peter McNab centered for Mel Bridgman and Rich Preston

Q6. Billy MacMillan became coach of the franchise when the team played in Denver. Name the skipper (above) he succeeded behind the bench.

NEW JERSEY DEVILS

Q40. This Devil captain is on record for scoring the quickest goal in Devil history. Name this sharpshooter.

Q53. This Devil was the first player taken in the 1975 draft. Who is he?

NEW JERSEY DEVILS

Q73. Name the referee who was the target of Jim Schoenfeld's infamous "doughnut tirade" after the Bruins knocked off the Devils, 6–1, in Game 3 of the 1988 Wales Conference Championship.

Q57 Before starring for the 1980 U.S. Olympic Team, Mark Johnson was taken in the 1977 draft. What club selected Johnson?

Q58 Name all of the Devils' team captains.

Q59 Name the Devil who served as an emergency replacement in the 1985 All-Star Game for Philadelphia's Brad Marsh when the Flyer was stranded by a blizzard.

Q60 Winger Pat Verbeek suffered a career-threatening injury in 1985 when he was involved in a farm accident. What happened to Verbeek?

Q61 Name the Devil center who led the NCAA in scoring from that hotbed of hockey, Northern Arizona University.

Q62 Who was the first Devil honored as the NHL Player of the Week, for the week ending November 1, 1986?

Q63 This Devil, who was a member of Montreal's 1986 Cup-winning team, won the Hobey Baker Award as the top U.S. collegiate player in 1984. Who is this University of Minnesota product?

Q64 Reijo Ruotsalainen played with Bern of the Swiss League for part of the 1986–87 season and again in 1988–89. The Finnish native also spent part of the 1986–87 campaign in North America. With what team did he play?

Q65 Which Devil standard does John McLean NOT hold?

(a) First Devil to score back-to-back hat tricks
(b) Scored OT goal that clinched Devils' first playoff berth
(c) Set team record for most assists by a right winger
(d) Most goals (four) in a game

Q66 Who was the first Devil to post 200-plus penalty minutes in three straight seasons and the first to record over 1,000 career penalty minutes?

NEW JERSEY DEVILS

A57 Pittsburgh Penguins (he was the team's third choice and the 66th player taken overall)

A58 Don Lever, Mel Bridgman, and Kirk Muller

A59 Phil Russell

A60 His left thumb was severed. It was reattached through microsurgery.

A61 Greg Adams

A62 Aaron Broten

A63 Tom Kurvers

A64 Edmonton Oilers

A65 (d)—Pat Verbeek holds the club record

A66 Ken Daneyko (1,051 PIM)

Q67 The Devils clinched their first-ever playoff spot by defeating Chicago in an April 1988 game. Who scored both the tying and winning goals in that contest?

Q68 Besides New Jersey, for what other NHL teams has Walt Poddubny played?

Q69 Who was in goal when the Devils chalked up their first playoff victory, a 3–2 decision against the Islanders on April 7, 1988?

Q70 Who scored the first playoff goal in Devil history in a division semifinal on April 6, 1988?

Q71 Who scored the game-winning shorthanded goal in Game 5 of the 1988 division semifinals?

Q72 Who set an NHL mark for most points (eight) in a playoff game?

Q73 Name the referee who was the target of Jim Schoenfeld's infamous "doughnut tirade" after the Bruins knocked off the Devils, 6–1, in Game 3 of the 1988 Wales Conference championship.

Q74 In what year did the Devils make the playoffs for the first time, and in what position did they finish?

Q75 The Devils' first overtime goal came in the second game of the 1988 conference championship series. Who scored at 17:46 of the fourth period?

Q76 The Devils won Game 7 of the 1988 division finals by downing the Capitals, 3–2, at Washington. Who scored the game-winner at 13:49 of the third period?

Q77 The Devils' first playoff win came in the second match of the 1988 playoffs. Who netted New Jersey's first postseason winning goal?

Q78 Three Devils registered hat tricks during the Washington series in 1988. Who were they?

Q79 Game 6 became a slugfest as the Devils lost at home, 7–2, and the series was knotted at three apiece. What Devil was hit with two game misconducts, a minor, a major, and game penalties totaling 37 minutes?

NEW JERSEY DEVILS

A67 John McLean

A68 Edmonton (1981–82), Toronto (1982–86), Rangers (1986–88), and Quebec (1988–89)

A69 Bob Sauve

A70 Craig Wolanin (he beat the Isles' Kelly Hrudey in the second period)

A71 Pat Conacher

A72 Patrik Sundstrom (against Washington in April 1988)

A73 Don Koharski

A74 The 1987–88 Devils were fourth-place finishers in the Patrick Division

A75 Rookie Doug Brown

A76 John McLean

A77 Mark Johnson

A78 Patrik Sundstrom, Aaron Broten, and Mark Johnson (Johnson had a four-goal game)

A79 Jim Korn

Q80   Why was Game 4 of the 1988 conference championship series delayed 66 minutes?

Q81   The Devils jumped to a two-games-to-one lead in the Patrick Division semifinals. Name the Capital forward who led his team with eight goals and brought them back to a 4–2 series victory.

TRADES, WAIVES, AND ACQUISITIONS

Q82   Whom did New Jersey claim from the Rangers in the 1982 NHL waiver draft?

Q83   The Devils' first trade took place on October 15, 1982. Name the four players exchanged between New Jersey and Hartford.

Q84   This former Devil and his brother were one of the highest drafted brother tandems in league history. Who are the talented siblings?

Q85   When Steve Tambellini and Joel Quenneville were shipped to Calgary in June 1983, whom did New Jersey acquire?

Q86   Who was the Devils' first choice, and the first overall selection, in the 1983 waiver draft?

Q87   Sean Burke was not the first player taken by the Devils in the 1985 entry draft. Who was?

Q88   Brendan Shanahan was the second overall choice in the 1987 entry draft. Who was chosen ahead of him?

Q89   Captain Mel Bridgman was traded in March 1987 for a third round draft choice in that season's entry draft and a Detroit player. Name the Red Wing.

Q90   How did the Devils obtain Walt Poddubny?

Q91   Quebec's Peter Stastny came to New Jersey at a dear price. Who was sent to the Nordiques in the transaction?

NEW JERSEY DEVILS

A80   The refs walked out in protest of the verbal abuse Jim Schoenfeld heaped on the referee in Game 1. Amateur officials were called in to work the game in their place.

A81   Dino Ciccarelli

—————————————— · ——————————————

A82   Carol Vadnais

A83   Rick Meagher and Garry Howatt came to the Devils for Merlin Malinowski and Scott Fusco

A84   Sylvain Turgeon (1983—second choice overall) and his brother Pierre (1987—first choice overall of the Buffalo Sabres)

A85   Mel Bridgman and Phil Russell

A86   Minnesota defenseman Murray Brumwell

A87   Craig Wolanin (he was selected with the third overall pick)

A88   Pierre Turgeon (by Buffalo)

A89   Chris Cichocki

A90   Poddubny came to New Jersey from Quebec in a trade for Joe Cirella and Claude Loiselle in June 1989

A91   Craig Wolanin and Randy Velischek

TRADES, WAIVES, AND ACQUISITIONS

Q92 Edmonton's Jeff Sharples missed out on being with a Stanley Cup winner when he was traded to the Devils in March 1990. Who was lucky enough to be sent to the NHL champions?

Q93 How did the Devils acquire high-scoring center Laurie Boschman the day before training camp 1990 opened?

NEW JERSEY DEVILS

A92 Reijo Ruotsalainen

A93 The Devils traded Bob Brooks to Winnipeg for Boschman

*** FAST FACTS ***

Club Records—Team

Most Points: 83 (1989–90)
Most Wins: 38 (1987–88)
Most Losses: 56 (1983–84)
Most Goals: 300 (1985–86)
Fewest Points: 41 (1983–84)
Fewest Wins: 17 (1982–83 and 1983–84)
Fewest Losses: 34 (1989–90)
Fewest Goals: 230 (1982–83)

Club Records—Individual

Most Seasons: Mike Kitchen and Aaron Broten, 8
Most Goals (career): Aaron Broten, 641
Most Points (career: Aaron Broten, 469 (162 goals, 307 assists)
Most Goals (season): Pat Verbeek, 47 (1987–88)
Most Points (season): Kirk Muller, 94 (1987–88: 37 goals, 57 assists)

New York Giants

NEW YORK GIANTS

1986 GIANTS

Row 1 2, Raul Allegre; 5, Sean Landeta; 15, Jeff Hostetler; 11, Phil Simms; Head Coach Bill Parcells, 53, Harry Carson, 17, Jeff Rutledge; 22, Lee Rouson, 23, Perry Williams

Row 2 24, Ottis Anderson; 25, Mark Collins; 27, Herb Welch; 30, Tony Galbreath; 33, George Adams; 34, Elvis Patterson; 39, Tyrone Davis; 43, Terry Kinard, 44, Maurice Carthon; 46, Greg Lasker; 20, Joe Morris

Row 3 Offensive Coordinator Ron Erhardt; 48, Kenny Hill; 51, Robbie Jones; 52, Pepper Johnson; 54, Andy Headen; 55, Gary Reasons; 56, Lawrence Taylor; 57, Byron Hunt; 58, Carl Banks; Defensive Coordinator Bill Belichick

Row 4 Receivers Coach Pat Hodgson; 59, Brian Johnston; 60, Brad Benson, 61, Chris Godfrey; 63, Karl Nelson; 64, Jim Burt; 65, Bart Oates; 66, William Roberts; 67, Billy Ard; Defensive Line Coach Lamar Leachman

Row 5 Tight Ends Coach Mike Pope; 78, Jerome Sally; 68, Damian Johnson; 69, David Jordan; 70, Leonard Marshall; 73, John Washington; 74, Erik Howard; 75, George Martin; 76, Curtis McGriff; 77, Eric Dorsey; Special Teams Coach Romeo Crennel

Row 6 Offensive Line Coach Fred Hoaglin; 80, Phil McConkey; 81, Stacy Robinson; 83, Vince Warren; 84, Zeke Mowatt; 86, Lionel Manuel; 87, Solomon Miller; 88, Bobby Johnson; 89, Mark Bavaro; Assistant Special Teams Coach Mike Sweatman; Strength and Conditioning Coach Johnny Parker

Row 7 Running Backs Coach Ray Handley; Field Sec. Mgr. Joe Mansfield; Asst. Film Coord. John Mancuso; Film Coord. Tony Ceglio; Locker Room Mgr. Ed Wagner; Asst. Equip. Mgr. Jim Phelan; Equipment Mgr. Ed Wagner, Jr.; Head Trainer Ronnie Barnes; Trainer Jim Madaleno; Trainer John Johnson; Head Trainer Emeritus John Dziegiel; Defensive Backfield Coach Len Fontes

- 246 -

THE SUITS

Q1 The original owner of the Giants, Tim Mara, worked in a profession that is now illegal. What did Mara do?

Q2 When Tim Mara purchased his franchise, the football league was already five years old. What was the league called?

Q3 Who was Dr. Harry March?

Q4 What four Giant head coaches have won the NFL championship?

Q5 Name the four Giant players who became head coach of the team.

Q6 What positions did the four play?

Q7 What two Giant coaches have been inducted into the Hall of Fame?

Q8 Who had the longest tenure as Giants head coach?

Q9 Name the two Giant coaches who were fired during the regular season.

Q10 Name the head coach who was fired between the last preseason game and the first regular-season game.

Q11 Name the Giant skipper who was best known as a professional wrestler and was fired as the Navy coach because of his foul temper.

Q12 When Tim Mara bought the Giants, it was almost an afterthought. What did he intend to do on that day in 1925?

Q13 The team's second skipper was a physician who practiced medicine during the week and coached on weekends (in 1925, he was the Giants' center). Name this single season head coach.

Q14 Steve Owen coached the Giants for 22 years. In his first season, he shared the team's reins with a player. Who was he?

Q15 Name the assistant coach who implemented the NFL's first T-formation.

Q16 How many Eastern Conference titles did Jim Lee Howell rack up from 1954 to 1960?

NEW YORK GIANTS

A1   He was a bookmaker

A2   The National Professional Football League

A3   March convinced Tim Mara to bring pro ball to New York. He was team secretary and eventually rose to the presidency of the club.

A4   Earl Potteiger (1927), Steve Owen (1934, 1938), Jim Lee Howell (1956), Bill Parcells (1986)

A5   Steve Owen (1931–53); Jim Lee Howell (1954–60); Alex Webster (1969–73); and player-coach Earl Potteiger (1927–28)

A6   Owen—tackle; Howell—end; Webster—back; Potteiger—back

A7   Vince Lombardi (1954–1958; assistant coach) and Steve Owen (1931–53; head coach)

A8   Steve Owen (1931–53)

A9   LeRoy Andrews (1930) and Bill Arnsparger (1976)

A10   Allie Sherman (after coaching from 1961 through 1968, he was fired when the Giants lost all five of their 1969 preseason games)

A11   Bob Folwell (1925)

A12   He was considering purchasing a percentage of pro fighter Gene Tunney's contract

A13   Dr. Joseph Alexander (1926: 8–4–1, .667 won-loss percentage)

A14   QB Benny Friedman (Friedman and Owen took over from LeRoy Andrews in mid-season)

A15   Allie Sherman

A16   Three

Q17 Seven of Jim Lee Howell's assistants became head coaches in the NFL. Name them.

Q18 In 1954, Jim Lee Howell hired an offensive coach who introduced the power sweep and double-team blocking. Who was responsible for these revolutionary tactics?

Q19 Who was at the helm when the Giants won three straight Eastern Conference titles—1961 through 1963?

Q20 Who was the only coach to register a winning season with the Giants during the 1970s?

Q21 Bill Arnsparger coached the Giants at three different home sites. Name the stadiums.

Q22 John McVay (1976–78) played under two of college football's greatest coaches while attending Miami of Ohio. Name his mentors.

Q23 John McVay replaced Bill Arnsparger as head coach seven games into the 1976 season. What team had McVay led prior to the Giants?

Q24 When Ray Perkins played at Alabama, three future NFL quarterbacks were also at the school. Name the 'Bama QBs.

Q25 Prior to his tenure in New York, with what two pro teams had Ray Perkins coached?

Q26 Whom did GM George Young replace in the Giants' front office on Valentine's Day, 1979?

Q27 What team drafted Bill Parcells as a linebacker in the early 1960s?

Q28 At what college was Bill Parcells head coach for one year?

Q29 Name the AFC team that employed Bill Parcells as a linebacking coach in 1980.

Q30 The New York franchise is one of three teams from the 1925 league still in existence in the same metropolitan area. What are the other two?

NEW YORK GIANTS

A17   Vince Lombardi (Green Bay/Washington), Tom Landry (Dallas), Dick Nolan (New Orleans/San Francisco), Harland Svare (San Diego), Alex Webster (Giants), Bill Austin (Pittsburgh/Washington), and Ed Hughes (Houston)

A18   Vince Lombardi

A19   Allie Sherman

A20   Alex Webster (1970: 9–5; 1972: 8–6)

A21   Yale Bowl, Shea Stadium, and Giants Stadium

A22   Woody Hayes and Ara Parseghian

A23   Memphis Southmen of the World Football League

A24   Joe Namath, Steve Sloan, and Ken Stabler

A25   New England Patriots (1974–1977: receiver coach); San Diego Chargers (1978: offensive coordinator)

A26   Andy Robustelli (who was director of operations)

A27   Detroit Lions

A28   Air Force Academy (1978)

A29   New England Patriots

A30   Chicago Bears and Green Bay Packers

Q31 How many times have the Giants gone from first to last in their division/conference in successive seasons?

Q32 What is the longest streak of consecutive winning seasons registered by the Giants?

Q33 What is the longest streak of consecutive losing seasons registered by the Giants?

Q34 The Giants have won their division 16 times since the club's inception. Name the only team to win more.

Q35 Name the three teams that have scored nine or more touchdowns in a game against the Giants.

Q36 Why was the Giants' December 6, 1925, game called "the loss that saved the franchise"?

Q37 The 1927 Giants were one of the greatest defensive teams in NFL history. In their 13-game schedule, how many times did they whitewash their opponent?

Q38 In 1930, the Giants played an exhibition game against a college football team to benefit the unemployed in New York City. What school did they play?

Q39 Harry Newman led the NFL in passing in the 1933 season because of a rule that was implemented that year. What rule revolutionized the game?

Q40 In 1939, the first Pro Bowl was played between the NFL champion Giants and the Pro All-Stars. Where was the contest played?

Q41 Whom were the Giants playing when news of the Pearl Harbor attack was announced at the Polo Grounds (December 7, 1941)?

Q42 It wasn't the thrill of victory or the agony of defeat at the Giants' farewell game at the Polo Grounds in 1955. What team did New York tie, 35–35?

Q43 Name the only team the Giants defeated in their dismal 1–12–1 season of 1966.

NEW YORK GIANTS

A31 Three times (1946 and 1947, 1963 and 1964, 1986 and 1987)

A32 10 seasons (1954–1963)

A33 Eight seasons (1973–1980)

A34 Cleveland Browns (18 division titles)

A35 Chicago Cardinals (1948: nine TDs), Pittsburgh Steelers (1952: nine TDs) and Washington Redskins (1966: 10 TDs)

A36 The Polo Grounds was packed with fans eager to see Red Grange and the Chicago Bears (the Giants lost, 19–7)

A37 10 times

A38 Notre Dame (The Giants won 22–0 against the Knute Rockne team. It was the last game Rockne coached.)

A39 A player was allowed to throw a pass from anywhere behind the line of scrimmage. (Before that, the passer had to remain at least five yards behind the line.)

A40 L.A.'s Wrigley Field (New York won, 13–10)

A41 Brooklyn Dodgers (Brooklyn won, 21–7)

A42 Cleveland Browns (the Giants started playing their home games at Yankee Stadium)

A43 Washington Redskins (13–10 at home)

Q44 Because of a revamped NFL alignment, the Giants played in two different divisions between 1967 and 1969. Name the divisions that comprised the Eastern Conference.

Q45 What team defeated New York in the 1970 season finale and knocked the Giants out of playoff contention?

Q46 In what year did the team move to Giants Stadium?

Q47 Whom did the Giants play in their first game at East Rutherford, N.J.?

Q48 Who scored the first touchdown at Giants Stadium?

Q49 When the Giants switched stadiums, something else changed, too. What was it?

Q50 When the Giants defeated the Cowboys and the Jets beat Green Bay on the final weekend of the 1981 season, it marked an event that was unprecedented in New York football history. What happened?

Q51 Name the Atlanta Falcon who scooped up a fumble and ran 91 yards for the winning touchdown in the Giants' 1982 home opener.

Q52 Name the two kickers who tied a league record by booting four field goals against the Giants in a single quarter.

Q53 What three teams did the Giants play during the 1987 replacement games?

Q54 When Philadelphia defeated New York on November 20, 1988, it was the first and only time that an overtime game ended in a particular manner. How did the contest end?

Q55 In 1989, the Giants ranked second in the NFL for fewest points allowed during the regular season (252). What team was first?

THE UNIFORMS

Q56 Who is the first Giant to pass for 300 yards in a game?

NEW YORK GIANTS

A44 1967 and 1969: Century Division; 1968: Capitol Division

A45 L.A. Rams (the loss resulted in Dallas winning the Eastern Division title)

A46 1976

A47 Dallas Cowboys (October 10, 1976: Dallas won, 24–14)

A48 Dallas's Robert Newhouse

A49 The team logo (it was changed from "NY" to "Giants")

A50 It was the first time both Big Apple teams entered the playoffs in the same year

A51 Bob Glazebrook

A52 Washington's Curt Knight (November 15, 1970) and Dallas's Roger Ruzek (November 2, 1987)

A53 San Francisco (49ers won, 41–21), Washington (Skins won, 38–12), and Buffalo (Bills won, 6–3)

A54 The game ended on a blocked field goal that the kicking team recovered (Lawrence Taylor blocked the kick only to have the Eagles' Clyde Simmons recover the pigskin and go in for a touchdown)

A55 Denver Broncos (226 points)

————————————————— · —————————————————

A56 Paul Governali (November 19, 1947: 341 yards against Philadelphia)

Q57 How many Heismann Trophy winners have played for the Giants?

Q58 Who is the last player to lead the team in both rushing and passing yardage in the same season?

Q59 What players teamed up to introduce the "alley oop pass"?

Q60 Who is the first Giant to reach the 1,000-yard mark in receptions?

Q61 Three players have led the Giants in rushing for four consecutive seasons. Name them.

Q62 Only three Giants have rushed for more than 1,000 yards in a season. Name them.

Q63 Who were the Baby Bulls?

Q64 Who is the only Giant to lead the NFL in rushing twice?

Q65 Which Giant was the first player in the NFL to see action in the Pro Bowl on both offense and defense?

Q66 Name the three Giants who have been selected MVP of the Pro Bowl.

Q67 Name the former Giant kicker who is the only man to score points in the AAFC, NFC, and AFL.

Q68 Name the three Giant quarterbacks enshrined in the Hall of Fame.

Q69 Of the 13 Giants who have entered the Hall of Fame, what three players spent their entire career with the New York team?

Q70 Name the rookie who led the NFL in 1964 with an average of 29.0 yards per kickoff return.

Q71 Since the AFL/NFL merger, no Giant has led the NFL in receiving, but two players have topped the NFC in catches. Name the New York leaders.

Q72 One of the best booters in the game, this Giant was known as "the Toeless Wonder" because he had just one toe on his kicking foot. Who was he?

NEW YORK GIANTS

A57   None

A58   Frank Filchock (1946)

A59   Y. A. Tittle and R. C. Owens

A60   Del Shofner (1961: 1,125 yards)

A61   Tuffy Leemans (1938–41), Frank Gifford (1956–59), and Joe Morris (1985–88)

A62   Ron Johnson (1970 and 1972), Joe Morris (1985, 1986, and 1988), and O. J. Anderson (1989)

A63   The 1965 backfield consisting of Tucker Frederickson, Ernie Koy, and Chuck Mercein

A64   Bill Paschal (1943: 572 yards; 1944: 737 yards)

A65   Frank Gifford (1953: defense; 1954: offense)

A66   Frank Gifford (1959), Sam Huff (1961), and Phil Simms (1986)

A67   Ben Agajanian (he played for Pittsburgh, the L.A. Dons, the L.A. Rams, the Washington Redskins, and the Dallas Texans)

A68   Arnie Herber (1944–45), Y. A. Tittle (1961–64), and Fran Tarkenton (1967–71)

A69   Roosevelt Brown, Frank Gifford, and Tuffy Leemans

A70   Clarence Childs (34 returns, 987 yards, one TD)

A71   Bob Tucker (1971: 59 catches) and Earnest Gray (1983: 78 catches)

A72   Ben Agajanian (1949, 1954–57)

Q73 What Giant booter earned a master's degree in Russian history from the University of Arkansas?

Q74 What Giant was the first defender to make the cover of *Time* magazine?

Q75 What two Giants have won Olympic gold medals?

Q76 At age 78, what Giant end was the oldest inductee into the Hall of Fame?

Q77 What Giant published a book on his favorite hobby, needlepoint?

Q78 What fabled skipper coached Giant quarterback Benny Friedman at Michigan?

Q79 Name the Giant kicker who was born with his right foot backward.

Q80 How many games did Jim Thorpe play as a Giant?

Q81 Name the player who was the first to sign with the Giants organization.

Q82 What was Bob Nash's claim to fame on the Giants team of 1925?

Q83 The NFL's first official pass reception leader was a Giant who caught 21 passes in 1932. Who was he?

Q84 The first Giant to rush for 100 yards in a game did so in 1933 against the Boston Braves. Name the ball carrier.

Q85 Name the Giant running back who led the NFL in rushing in his rookie season.

NEW YORK GIANTS

A73 Pat Summerall

A74 Sam Huff (1960)

A75 Jim Thorpe (1912) and Henry Carr (1964)

A76 Red Badgro (1981)

A77 Roosevelt (Rosey) Grier

A78 Fielding "Hurry Up" Yost

A79 Pat Summerall (in a historic operation, doctors broke Summerall's right leg and turned his foot around)

A80 Two games

A81 Jim Thorpe

A82 He was the first captain of the team

A83 Ray Flaherty

A84 Harry Newman

A85 Tuffy Leemans (1936: 836 yards)

THE UNIFORMS

Q86 What Giant halfback went on to become a major league baseball umpire after he coached a professional basketball team?

Q87 This famous Mississippi football family had three sons who played end for the Giants in different eras: 1937–41 and 1946; 1947–52; and 1954–55. Who were the talented siblings?

Q88 An All-Pro in 1939 and an assistant coach in the late 1950s, this Giant was bumped from center to guard because of Mel Hein's dominance in the middle. Who was he?

Q89 What was Tuffy Leemans's real first name?

Q90 The Giants won the 1944 Eastern Division title with the help of two players who were lured out of retirement. Name the men involved.

Q91 Name the two Giants who died in World War II.

Q92 What two Giants were suspended from the NFL in 1946 for alleged gambling activity?

Q93 Defensive back Tom Landry came to the Giants when the All-American Football Conference folded in 1949. With what team did he play prior to joining the Giants?

Q94 In the 1950s, New York was the first team to employ the umbrella defense. Name the four players who comprised that defensive backfield.

Q95 The first NFL Pro Bowl in its present format (the best players from each conference playing each other) was played in 1951. Name the seven Giants who dominated the East roster.

Q96 Choo Choo Roberts left the Giants to play in a newly formed league in 1951. To what league did he jump?

Q97 Who replaced Choo Choo in the Giant backfield?

Q98 In 1952, defensive back Emlen Tunnell gained more yards on kick returns and interceptions (924 yards) than the league's leading runner. Who was the NFL's leading rusher that season?

NEW YORK GIANTS

A86   Hank Soar (Giants: 1937–44, 1946; Providence Steamrollers basketball team: 1947–48; American League umpire: 1950–71)

A87   Jim, Ray, and Barney Poole

A88   Johnny Dell Isola

A89   Alphonse

A90   Arnie Herber and Ken Strong

A91   John Lummus and Al Blozis (a total of 55 Giants served in the war)

A92   Frankie Filchock and Merle Hapes

A93   The New York Yankees

A94   Otto Schnellbacher, Emlen Tunnell, Tom Landry, and Harmon Rowe

A95   Emlen Tunnell, Al DeRogatis, Charlie Conerly, Gene Roberts, Arnie Weinmeister, John Cannady, and Otto Schnellbacher

A96   Canadian Football League

A97   Kyle Rote

A98   L.A.'s Dan Towler (894 yards)

Q99   This nine-time Pro Bowl tackle was a 27th-round selection in the 1953 draft. Who is this Morgan State graduate?

Q100   Nicknamed "the Claw from Kansas," this Giant defensive back is the only player to lead two leagues in interceptions—the All-American Football Conference in 1948 and the NFL in 1951. Name him.

Q101   What is linebacker Sam Huff's real first name?

Q102   Rosey Grier spent seven seasons in a Giant uniform but missed all of the 1957 season. Why?

Q103   Pat Summerall demonstrated his true value as a Giant kicker for three seasons (1958–61). For what other NFL clubs did he play?

Q104   What Giant scored Notre Dame's winning touchdown and ended Oklahoma's 47-game winning skein during the 1950s?

Q105   Joe Morrison played with the Giants from 1959 until 1972. In that time, he played six different positions with the team. Name the positions.

Q106   What player accounted for a stunning 31.6 percent of the Giants' points in 1959?

Q107   What Hall of Fame receiver did the Giants cut in 1959 because "he had bad hands"?

Q108   Who hosted the 1960 documentary *The Violent World of Sam Huff*?

Q109   Name the two Giants who returned interceptions for 100-plus yards during the 1960s.

Q110   In 1961, Frank Gifford retired from football after he was knocked senseless by an Eagle in a mid-season game the previous year. Who put the hit on Gifford?

Q111   When Gifford retired in 1961, two players rotated to fill his position. Name them.

Q112   Who replaced Pat Summerall as the Giants' place-kicker in 1962?

NEW YORK GIANTS

A99   Roosevelt Brown

A100   Otto Schnellbacher

A101   Robert (his full name is Robert Lee Huff)

A102   He was in the military

A103   Chicago Cardinals and Detroit Lions

A104   Dick Lynch

A105   Flanker, split end, tight end, fullback, halfback, and safety

A106   Pat Summerall

A107   Don Maynard

A108   Walter Cronkite

A109   Erich Barnes (1961: 102 yards against Dallas) and Henry Carr (1966: 101 yards against L.A. Rams)

A110   Chuck Bednarik (Gifford resumed his career in 1962 and played through the 1964 season)

A111   Del Shofner and Joe Walton

A112   Don Chandler

THE UNIFORMS

Q113 When the Football Hall of Fame opened in 1963, five Giants were charter inductees. Name the quintet.

Q114 Name the Hall of Fame running back who played the 1963 season with the Giants before hanging up his cleats for good.

—YAT—

Q115 The Giants obtained Y. A. Tittle from the San Francisco 49ers in 1960. Whom did New York send to the West Coast in return?

Q116 What two QBs replaced Y. A. Tittle in the 49er lineup when the team shipped him to the Giants in 1961?

Q117 How old was Y.A. Tittle when the Giants acquired him in 1961?

Q118 Y. A. Tittle led the Giants 1961–64, and Fran Tarkenton was the field general 1967–1971. Name the quarterbacks in the interim years, 1965 and 1966.

Q119 With whom did Y. A. Tittle share the 1963 MVP award?

Q120 Against what team did Y. A. Tittle tie an NFL record for TD passes when he threw seven in one game during the 1962 season?

Q121 Y. A. Tittle matched the pro record for single-season TD passes by throwing 36 in 1963. Whose mark did he equal?

Q122 It would take 21 years for a player to overtake Tittle's TD passing mark. Name the QB who finally exceeded 36 scoring passes in a season.

Q123 For what two teams did Tittle play prior to arriving in New York?

Q124 What does the "Y. A." stand for in Y. A. Tittle?

Q125 Whom did the Bald Eagle replace as the starting QB in the Giants 1961 lineup?

NEW YORK GIANTS

A113   Owner Tim Mara, Mel Hein, Wilbur Henry, Cal Hubbard, and Jim Thorpe

A114   Hugh McElhenny ("Hurryin' Hugh" was 34 years old in 1963)

A115   Lou Cordileone

A116   John Brodie and Billy Kilmer

A117   35 years old

A118   Earl Morrall (1965), Gary Wood and Tom Kennedy (1966)

A119   Cleveland's Jim Brown

A120   Washington Redskins (he also had 505 yards in the 49–34 win)

A121   Houston's George Blanda (1961)

A122   Dan Marino (1984: 48 TDs; he did it again in 1986, when he threw 44 TD strikes)

A123   The Baltimore Colts (1948–50: All-American Football Conference and NFL) and the San Francisco '49ers (1951–60)

A124   Yelverton Abraham

A125   Charlie Conerly and his backup George Shaw

THE UNIFORMS

Q126 Rosey Grier was a member of two "Fearsome Foursomes." Name the New York and Los Angeles units.

Q127 What defensive back left the team in 1966 to sign with the Oakland Raiders, and then returned to the Giants the following season?

Q128 Pete Gogolak, the NFL's first soccer-style kicker, came to the Giants in 1966 after he left an AFL team. From what team did he defect?

Q129 Name the former Giant who kicked the first PAT in Super Bowl history.

Q130 For what three NFL teams did Earl Morrall play prior to his three-year stint with the Giants (1965–67)?

Q131 Whom did Frank Gifford replace in the *Monday Night Football* booth after the show's first season (1970)?

Q132 In the same season this running back started his pro career with the Giants, his brother was winning the American League batting championship with the California Angels. Name the Giant.

Q133 This 1970 first-round draft pick played only four seasons before he retired to become a minister. Name this Oklahoma linebacker.

Q134 What former Giant was an All–Big 10 pitcher in college and was offered $100,000 to play baseball for the St. Louis Cardinals?

Q135 For 11 seasons (1974–84), Dave Jennings distinguished himself as one of the league's premier punters. Whom did he succeed in that position?

Q136 With what team did Larry Csonka play prior to joining New York in 1976?

Q137 What wide receiver did Craig Morton hook up with to score the first Giant TD in the Meadowlands on October 10, 1976?

Q138 For what team did QB Joe Pisarcik play before he joined the Giants in 1977?

Q139 The number one pick from tiny Morehead State, Phil Simms joined New York in 1979. Who is the only other NFLer to come from that Kentucky school?

NEW YORK GIANTS

A126   Giants: Grier, Dick Modzelewski, Jim Katcavage, and Andy Robustelli; Rams: Grier, Deacon Jones, Merlin Olsen, and Lamar Lundy

A127   Willie Williams (1965, 1967–73)

A128   The Buffalo Bills

A129   Don Chandler (1967: for the Green Bay Packers)

A130   San Francisco, Pittsburgh, and Detroit

A131   Keith Jackson (Giff teamed with Howard Cosell and Don Meredith)

A132   Ron Johnson (his brother Alex won the batting crown in 1970)

A133   Jim Files

A134   Brad Van Pelt

A135   Tom Blanchard

A136   Memphis of the World Football League

A137   Jimmy Robinson (1976–79)

A138   Calgary of the CFL

A139   Gary Shirk

*** FAST FACTS ***

Giant Individual Records—Career

Rushing: Joe Morris, 5,296 yards (1982–88)
Passing (yards): Phil Simms, still active (1979–)
Receiving (yards): Frank Gifford, 5,434 (1952–60; 1962–64)

Q15. Name the New York assistant coach who implemented the NFL's first T-formation.

NEW YORK GIANTS

Q115. The Giants obtained Y. A. Tittle from the San Francisco 49ers in 1960. Whom did New York send to the West Coast in return?

Q247. Emlen Tunnell held the NFL interception record until 1979. Who surpassed his total of career pickoffs?

Q140 Phil Simms was the runner-up in the 1979 Rookie of the Year balloting. Who won the award?

Q141 Name the Giant running back who died of a brain tumor during the 1982 season.

Q142 What pro baseball team drafted Jeff Rutledge out of high school?

Q143 Who were the two Giants named to the All-NFL Rookie team in 1982, the year of the players' strike?

Q144 This Giant star shone brightly in a 1982 Monday night contest when he chalked up 20 solo tackles and five assists. Name the player.

Q145 When Phil Simms went down with a knee injury in 1982, who moved into the starting quarterback role?

Q146 Name the QB who was acquired in 1982 to fill the role of backup quarterback when Simms was injured.

Q147 Phil Simms set a club record by throwing for 513 yards on October 13, 1985. Against what team did he put on the aerial display?

Q148 In his first season out of Clemson, Terry Kinard alternated at safety with a veteran DB before displacing him completely. Name the player Kinard eventually replaced.

Q149 Zeke Mowatt, who signed with the Giants in 1983, was a little-known free agent until he knocked off two veteran tight ends for the starting job. Who were the two displaced Giants?

Q150 Whom did Ali Haji-Sheikh beat out for a job on the Giants' 1983 roster?

Q151 In the second game of the 1985 season, kicker Ali Haji-Sheikh pulled a hamstring and was lost for the season. Name the two players who replaced him for the balance of the year.

Q152 In this linebacker's first game, he registered 10 solo tackles, two QB sacks, and a fumble recovery and was named *Sports Illustrated*'s Player of the Week. Name him.

Q153 Joe Morris was used only sparingly in his first two years with New York, but in 1984 he became the starting running back. Whom did he replace in the backfield?

NEW YORK GIANTS

A140   Ottis Anderson (with St. Louis at the time)

A141   Doug Kotar (1974–82)

A142   Chicago Cubs (Rutledge opted for a football scholarship to Alabama instead, even though his father, Paul "Jack" Rutledged, had played with the Cubs)

A143   Rich Umphrey and Butch Woolfolk

A144   Harry Carson (against Green Bay)

A145   Scott Brunner (1980–83)

A146   Jeff Rutledge (from Los Angeles)

A147   Cincinnati (the Bengals won, 35–30)

A148   Beasley Reece

A149   Gary Shirk and Tom Mullady

A150   Joe Danelo

A151   Jesse Atkinson (six games) and Eric Schubert (eight regular season games and two postseason)

A152   Carl Banks (October 14, 1984: Giants defeated Atlanta, 19–7)

A153   Butch Woolfolk

Q154   A three-year veteran of the USFL Philadelphia/Baltimore Stars, Sean Landeta wrested the punting job in 1985 from this Giant kicker. Whom did Landeta replace?

Q155   Name the three defensive players who registered double-digit sacks in the 1985 season.

Q156   Whom did Mark Bavaro replace as the starting tight end in the 1985 Giants' lineup?

Q157   Veteran QB Jeff Rutledge had just one completion in all of 1986: a 13-yard pass on a fake field goal against the Eagles. Who caught it?

Q158   New York used three different starting quarterbacks during the 1987 replacement games. Who were the field generals?

Q159   In the 1988 season opener, the two previous Super Bowl winners (Giants and Redskins) met. The game was ultimately determined by back-to-back defensive TDs. Name the Giants who scored the winning points.

Q160   What Giant broke Walter Payton's collegiate career rushing record at Jackson State?

Q161   Pepper Johnson got his nickname when his aunt noticed him sprinkling the seasoning on a dish. What food did Johnson pepper?

Q162   With what team did Maurice Carthon begin his professional career?

Q163   O. J. Anderson is an alumnus of the University of Miami. Whose career rushing record did he surpass at the school?

Q164   How many 1,000-yard rushing seasons has Ottis Anderson had in his career?

Q165   What player has been with the present Giants the longest?

Q166   How many sacks did Lawrence Taylor have in his rookie year?

Q167   It wasn't until L.T.'s final year at North Carolina that he played outside linebacker/defensive end. What position did the All-American play before?

NEW YORK GIANTS

A154   Dave Jennings

A155   Leonard Marshall (15.5), Lawrence Taylor (13), and George Martin (10)

A156   Zeke Mowatt (Mowatt was lost for the year when he suffered a serious knee injury in the preseason)

A157   Harry Carson

A158   Jim Crocicchia, Mike Busch, and Jeff Rutledge

A159   Tom Flynn returned a blocked punt 27 yards and Jim Burt returned a fumble 39 yards in New York's 27–20 victory

A160   Lewis Tillman (3,989 yards)

A161   Breakfast cereal

A162   New Jersey Generals (he played with the Generals 1983–85)

A163   Chuck Foreman (Anderson was also the first 'Cane to break the 1,000-yard rushing mark in a season)

A164   Six (as of the end of the 1989 season)

A165   Phil Simms (who was drafted in 1979)

A166   Nine and a half (1981)

A167   Nose guard

Q168   Lawrence Taylor had 105 tackles, 20 1/2 QB sacks, three forced fumbles, and a 34-yard TD interception return in 1986. Taylor was the hands-down winner of the NFL's MVP award, and the first defensive player in a decade to capture the award. What other defensive standout won the award in 1976?

Q169   Lawrence of the Meadowlands set a record for the longest interception by a linebacker in team history. How many yards did he scamper in the record-setting return?

Q170   Lawrence Taylor was one of three players who were unanimous selections for the NFL's All-1980s team. Who are the other two?

Q171   Match the player with his retired uniform number:

(a) Al Blozis	1
(b) Charlie Conerly	7
(c) Ray Flaherty	14
(d) Mel Hein	32
(e) Joe Morrison	40
(f) Ken Strong	42
(g) Y. A. Tittle	50

GLORY DAYS

Q172   The Giants have played in 17 NFL championship contests. What team have they met the most times in the title games?

Q173   Only one club has a poorer winning percentage in NFC championship games than the Giants. Name the team.

Q174   In the 1934 championship, who scored the game's first and the Bears' only TD?

Q175   Frank Filchock set a league record for interceptions thrown in an NFL championship game. How many did he throw in the Giants' loss to the Bears in 1946?

Q176   The Giants defeated Chicago for the 1956 NFL title by a score of 47–7. Who scored the Bears' only touchdown?

NEW YORK GIANTS

A168 Minnesota Viking Alan Page

A169 97 (November 25, 1982: against Detroit)

A170 Anthony Muñoz and Jerry Rice

A171 (a) 32, (b) 42, (c) 1, (d) 7, (e) 40, (f) 50, (g) 14

A172 Chicago Bears (New York has won two and lost five)

A173 Tampa Bay (New York is 4–11, while Tampa is 0–1)

A174 Bronco Nagurski (New York won, 30–13)

A175 Six interceptions

A176 Rich Casares

GLORY DAYS

—The 1958 Championship Game—

Q177 What team did the Giants defeat in back-to-back games in order to win the 1958 Eastern Division title?

Q178 Name the only other team to win the NFL's Eastern Conference between 1958 and 1963 besides the Giants.

Q179 The 1958 NFL championship was the first sudden-death overtime game in league history. Who were the opposing head coaches?

Q180 In the 1958 championship game, the Giants' first TD was the result of an 86-yard gain on the previous down. What three players handled the ball on the broken play?

Q181 What Colt broke his leg with less than three minutes left in the game and New York holding on to a 17–14 lead?

Q182 With seven seconds left in regulation, Baltimore booted the tying field goal from 13 yards out. Who was the kicker on the play?

Q183 New York won the toss and took the kickoff in the overtime period. Who caught the kickoff and returned it to the Giants' 20-yard line?

Q184 The final score of the contest was 23–17 as the Colts scored on a one-yard run after 8:15 of overtime had elapsed. Who carried the ball on the winning rush?

_____ · _____

Q185 The 1959 championship game saw a rematch of the teams that played in the 1958 contest. What two Giants accounted for all of New York's points in the game?

Q186 After taking a 9–7 lead into the fourth quarter of the 1959 championship game, the Giants were mauled for 24 points before losing the game 31–16. What Colt cornerback intercepted Charlie Conerly twice in the last period, including a 42-yard pickoff for a TD?

Q187 In the 1962 NFL championship against the Packers, the Giants' only score came on an end-zone recovery of a blocked punt. Name the two Giants involved in the scoring play.

Q188 In the 1962 NFC championship game, Sam Huff did something to Packer Jim Taylor that will live in infamy. What did Huff do in New York's 16–7 loss?

NEW YORK GIANTS

———————————— · ————————————

A177 Cleveland Browns (the first win tied the teams in the regular season and the second victory gave New York the title)

A178 Philadelphia Eagles (1960)

A179 New York: Jim Lee Howell; Baltimore: Weeb Ewbank

A180 Charlie Conerly, Kyle Rote, Alex Webster (Conerly passed from his own 13 to Rote; Rote ran to the 24-yard line, fumbled, and the ball was picked up by Webster, who carried it to the Colts' one-yard line)

A181 Gino Marchetti (when his teammate Gene "Big Daddy" Lipscomb fell on him as he was tackling Frank Gifford)

A182 Steve Myhra

A183 Don Maynard

A184 Alan Ameche

———————————— · ————————————

A185 Pat Summerall (three FGs) and Bob Schnelker (TD reception)

A186 Johnny Sample

A187 Erich Barnes blocked the punt, and Jim Collier recovered the ball for a TD

A188 Huff bit Taylor through his helmet

Q189 Name the Green Bay kicker in the 1962 championship game who kicked three field goals against New York.

Q190 In the 1963 championship game between New York and the Bears, Y. A. Tittle was knocked out in the first half with a wrenched knee. Who replaced the Bald Eagle for part of the game?

Q191 Name the Bear who temporarily knocked the 37-year-old Tittle out of the championship game.

Q192 The Giants made the playoffs in 1981 by defeating the Eagles, 27–21, in the NFC's wild-card game. When was the last time New York won a postseason game before this victory?

Q193 The Giants met San Francisco in a divisional playoff game on January 3, 1982. A fight in the fourth quarter ended an attempt by New York to stage a comeback, and the 49ers went on to win 38–24. What two players were involved in the fracas?

Q194 New York defeated L.A. in the 1984 wild-card game, 16–13. Who was the only Giant to score a TD in the contest?

Q195 The Giants met the eventual winner of Super Bowl XIX, the 49ers, in the 1984 divisional playoffs. Who scored New York's only TD in the 21–10 loss?

Q196 On San Francisco's final TD drive in that contest, a debatable late-hit call resulted in a 31-yard gain for the 49ers. Against what Giant was the flag thrown?

Q197 The eventual Super Bowl XX winners, the Bears, defeated New York, 21–0, in the 1985 NFC divisional playoffs. Their first score came on a Sean Landeta fumble after he missed his footing and dropped the ball. Who recovered the fumble for a TD?

Q198 New York's best scoring chance in the 1985 divisional playoff game came with less than a minute left in the half and the Giants at the Bear two-yard line with first-and-goal. Who dropped a sure TD pass from Simms?

—Super Bowl XXI—

Q199 Name the only team to score against the Giants in the NFC 1986 playoffs.

Q200 What NFC teams did New York defeat in order to reach the Super Bowl?

NEW YORK GIANTS

A189 Jerry Kramer

A190 Glynn Griffing (Tittle, although barely able to walk, played the entire second half)

A191 Larry Morris

A192 1958 (when New York defeated Cleveland in a playoff game)

A193 Gary Jeter threw a punch at 49er Dan Audick (At the time, New York was down 24–17, but had San Francisco in a third-and-18 situation. The penalty gave the 49ers a first down, and they went on to score a touchdown.)

A194 Rod Carpenter (one-yard run; the Rams' only TD was a 14-yard scamper by Eric Dickerson)

A195 Harry Carson (on a 14-yard interception return)

A196 Bill Currier (on a hit to WR Freddie Soloman)

A197 Chicago's Sean Gayle

A198 Bobby Johnson

A199 The 49ers (the Giants won, 49–3)

A200 San Francisco (49–3) and Washington (17–0)

Q201 One of the greatest Giant teams was the 1986 club, as they registered 12 straight wins, a 10–0 record at home, a 14–2 season record, and a romp over the Broncos in the Super Bowl. During their playoff steamroll, what NFL playoff record did the team establish?

Q202 What was the site of Super Bowl XXI on January 25, 1987?

Q203 Who scored the first points in Super Bowl XXI?

Q204 Who scored New York's first touchdown in the game?

Q205 The only score in the second quarter was a safety. Name the tackler and the ballcarrier on the play.

Q206 With New York down 10–9 in the third quarter, Coach Parcells decided to go on fourth and a half-yard at his own 46. Who carried the ball for the first down?

Q207 In the Giants' victory over Denver in Super Bowl XXI, Phil Simms completed 22 of 25 passes for an amazing 88 percent. That is the highest completion percentage in postseason history (minimum: 15 attempts). Whose record did Simms surpass?

Q208 Who passed for more yardage in the game: Simms or Elway?

Q209 What two Super Bowl passing records did Phil Simms establish?

Q210 What was the final score of the game?

Q211 What Bronco led his team in rushing yardage for the game?

Q212 Who was the game's MVP?

———————————— · ————————————

Q213 The Giants lost 19–13 in overtime in the 1989 playoff game against the Rams. Who scored New York's only TD of the game?

Q214 On the tying drive by L.A., an apparent interception was ruled an incomplete pass, which allowed the Rams to kick a 22-yard field goal. What Giant thought he had picked off Jim Everett's pass?

NEW YORK GIANTS

A201 The Giants set a record composite margin of victory in the playoffs, outscoring their three opponents, 105–23

A202 Rose Bowl, Pasadena, California

A203 Denver's Rich Karlis (48-yard field goal)

A204 Zeke Mowatt (on a six-yard pass from Simms)

A205 George Martin sacked John Elway

A206 Jeff Rutledge (The Giants shifted out of punt formation and the reserve QB moved from upback to quarterback. The Giants scored a touchdown and took a lead they never lost.)

A207 Miami's David Woodley's (1/8/83: vs. New England in the AFC first-round game, 84.2 percent)

A208 John Elway (304 yards against Simms's 268 yards)

A209 Highest completion percentage (88 percent) and consecutive completions (10)

A210 39–20

A211 John Elway (six attempts, 27 yards)

A212 Phil Simms

——————————— · ———————————

A213 Ottis Anderson (two-yard run)

A214 Perry Williams

Q215 The game was lost on a questionable pass interference call in the overtime period that gave L.A. a 27-yard pickup to the Giant 25. On whom was the flag thrown?

Q216 Name the two Andersons who scored all of the touchdowns in the Giants–Rams 1989 postseason game.

—Super Bowl XXV—

Q217 With San Francisco leading 13-9 in the 1991 championship game, the Giants faked a punt in the fourth quarter, gained a first down, and ultimately scored a field goal. Who gained 30 yards on the fourth down play?

Q218 "Threepeat" was thwarted when Roger Craig fumbled in the fourth quarter and Matt Bahr kicked a 42-yard field goal as time expired. Name the Giant who forced Craig's fumble and the player who recovered the ball for New York.

Q219 Steve Young mopped up for the 49ers after Joe Montana suffered a broken hand, bruised sternum, and concussion with ten minutes left in the game. Who laid the hit on Montana?

Q220 How many Giants were on New York's roster for both Super Bowl XXI and Super Bowl XXV?

Q221 Four members of the Giants' 1990 team played in the Super Bowl with other clubs. Match the player with the team.

(A) Lawrence McGrew   (1) Pittsburgh (S.B. XIV)
(B) Dave Duerson   (2) S.F. 49ers (S.B. XIX)
(C) Matt Bahr   (3) Chicago (S.B. XX)
(D) Matt Cavanaugh   (4) New England (S.B. XX)

Q222 Name the Bills kicker who missed the 47-yard field goal with four seconds left in the game.

Q223 Super Bowl XXV was the closest game in the contest's history (20–19) and the second to be decided by a field goal. Name the only kicker besides Matt Bahr to score the games' winning points.

Q224 Jeff Hostetler is one of three backup quarterbakcs to lead his club to Super Bowl victory. Name the other two.

NEW YORK GIANTS

A215   Sheldon White (two plays later, Everett threw a 30-yard TD pass)

A216   New York: Ottis Anderson; L.A.: Flipper Anderson

A217   Gary Reasons (He ran from the Giants' 46-yard line to the 49er 24-yard line to set up the score.)

A218   Nose tackle Erik Howard caused the fumble and Lawrence Taylor recovered the ball at the New York 43-yard line.

A219   Leonard Marshall

A220   21 (Raul Allegre, Ottis Anderson, Carl Banks, Mark Bavaro, Maurice Carthon, Mark Collins, Eric Dorsey, Jeff Hostetler, Erik Howard, Pepper Johnson, Sean Landeta, Leonard Marshall, Bart Oates, Gary Reasons, Stacy Robinson, William Roberts, Lee Rouson, Phil Simms, Lawrence Taylor, John Washington, and Perry Wiliams)

A221   A—4, B—3, C—1, D—2.

A222   Scott Norwood

A223   Baltimore Colt Jim O'Brien (Super Bowl V—The Colts defeated Dallas on O'Brien's 32-yard kick with five seconds left.)

A224   Jim Plunkett (L.A. Raiders—1981) and Doug Williams (Redskins—1988)

Q225 Thirty-three-year-old Ottis Anderson was named the Super Bowl's MVP (21 carries, 102 yards; 4.9 yard average). Only two other MVPs were older when they were so honored. Name them.

Q226 Which record was NOT set or tied in Super Bowl XXV?

A. Longest time of possession by one team
B. Most field goals by both teams
C. Fewest turnovers by both teams
D. Fewest punt returns by both teams

SETTING THE STANDARD

Q227 The Giants once chalked up 62 points against an opponent. Whom did they defeat by a score of 62–10?

Q228 Only two quarterbacks have matched Phil Simms's feat of two consecutive 400-yard passing games (1985). Name them.

Q229 The longest pass play in Giant history occurred during the 1966 season and went for 98 yards. Name the quarterback and the receiver on the play.

Q230 Whose career team rushing record did Joe Morris surpass?

Q231 Who was the Giants' first 1,000-yard rusher?

Q232 The team record for the longest run from scrimmage, 91 yards, has stood since 1930. Who was the ballcarrier?

Q233 Who was the first Giant to have over 1,000 yards in receptions in a season?

Q234 Name the Giant who was the first tight end in NFL history to lead the league in receptions.

Q235 In 1966, the Giants and their opponent established an NFL record for points scored (113) by two teams in a single game. Whom were the Giants playing?

Q236 Name the Giant who set a team record for most fumbles in one season (1985).

NEW YORK GIANTS

A225 Bart Starr (34, Super Bowl II) and Len Dawson (34, Super Bowl IV)

A226 B (The records: A—New York: 40:33; C—0 turnovers; D—2: tying the Super Bowl XX record)

----------------------- · -----------------------

A227 Philadelphia Eagles (November 26, 1972)

A228 San Diego's Dan Fouts (1982) and Miami's Dan Marino (1984)

A229 Earl Morrall to Homer Jones

A230 Alex Webster's team record of 4,638 yards (Morris has 5,296 yards)

A231 Ron Johnson (1970: 1,027 yards)

A232 Hap Moran (November 23, 1930: against Green Bay)

A233 Del Shofner (1962: 1,181 yards)

A234 Bob Tucker (1971: 59 receptions)

A235 Washington Redskins (November 27, 1966; 'Skins won, 72–41)

A236 Phil Simms (16)

Q237 Name the former Giant who established an NFL record by recovering 43 fumbles in his career.

Q238 Who is the Giants' all-time field goal percentage leader?

Q239 Pat Summerall set a team mark when he booted 14 consecutive field goals during the 1961 season. Who broke his record by kicking 18 in a row?

Q240 In this kicker's debut, he booted five field goals and became the first player in league history to hit that many in his first pro appearance. Name the Giant.

Q241 What Giant set a record for consecutive punts without a blocked kick?

Q242 Emlen Tunnell set a club mark for single-season punt return yardage with 489 yards (1951). Who broke the Hall of Famer's record?

Q243 Who returned a punt for 83 yards in 1963—the longest in club history?

Q244 Name the Giant who holds the team record for career safeties.

Q245 The Giants were involved in the last 0–0 tie in the NFL. Name New York's opponent.

Q246 In 1951, Eddie Price set a league mark by carrying the ball 271 times during the season. Whose record did he shatter?

Q247 Emlen Tunnell held the NFL interception record until 1979. Who surpassed his total of 79 career interceptions?

Q248 Besides the loss of his interception record, Emlen Tunnell's standard for career punt return yardage was also broken in the 1979 season. Who eclipsed Tunnell in this category?

Q249 Only two quarterbacks have thrown for more interceptions in their careers than Fran Tarkenton. Name them.

Q250 Fran Tarkenton paid the price for his scrambling abilities—he holds the NFL record for career sacks. How many times did he go down behind the line of scrimmage?

Q251 George Martin holds the all-time NFL record for most TDs scored by a defensive lineman. What is his mark?

NEW YORK GIANTS

A237   Fran Tarkenton (all 43 were his own dropped balls)

A238   Raul Allegre (1986–88: 51 for 70—.729)

A239   Joe Danelo

A240   Eric Schubert (1985)

A241   Dave Jennings (1976–83: 623 punts)

A242   Dave Meggett (1989: 582 yards)

A243   Eddie Dove (against Philadelphia)

A244   Jim Katcavage (three)

A245   Detroit Lions (1943)

A246   Philadelphia's Steve Van Buren (1949: 263 attempts; Price's record was eclipsed only six years later by Jim Brown)

A247   Minnesota's Paul Krause

A248   Billy Johnson (3,317 yards in 14 years)

A249   George Blanda (277 interceptions) and John Hadl (268 interceptions)—Tarkenton has 266 interceptions

A250   483 times in his four-year career with New York

A251   Six

SETTING THE STANDARD

Q252 What team set a league record by registering three safeties in a game against New York in 1984?

Q253 Ottis Anderson had 14 rushing touchdowns for New York in 1989. Name the only Giant who ran for more TDs.

TRADES, WAIVES, AND ACQUISITIONS

Q254 How many times have the Giants had the number one overall pick in the collegiate draft, and whom did they select with the choices?

Q255 In 1929, Tim Mara had his eye on triple-threat quarterback Benny Friedman, but he was under contract to another team. In order to bring Friedman to New York, Mara bought the franchise and disbanded it. What club did the Giant owner purchase in the transaction?

Q256 The NFL's first collegiate draft took place in 1936. Whom did New York select with their top choice?

Q257 Name the 1955 first-round draft pick of the Giants who carried the ball eight times during the year, gained 29 yards, and, at season's end, quit pro football for good.

Q258 In 1955, Ram Andy Robustelli asked to be allowed to report late to training camp because his wife was pregnant. The coach refused the request and traded the defensive end to the Giants. Name the coach.

Q259 From what team was Pat Summerall acquired in 1958?

Q260 Who was traded to the Rams for tackle John LoVetere and a draft pick after the 1962 season?

Q261 In 1963, Sam Huff was shipped to Washington along with rookie guard George Seals in one of the organization's most controversial trades. Whom did the Giants receive in return?

Q262 In 1964, the Giants used their first-round draft pick to select Joe Don Looney, a running back from Oklahoma. What is significant about Looney's association with the Giants?

NEW YORK GIANTS

A252   L.A. Rams

A253   Joe Morris (1985: 21 TDs)

_____ · _____

A254   Three times; 1951: Kyle Rote (Southern Methodist), 1965: Tucker Frederickson (Auburn), 1968: traded to the Vikings as one of four picks for Tarkenton

A255   Detroit Wolverines

A256   Ohio University tackle Art Lewis

A257   Notre Dame's Joe Heap

A258   Sid Gillman

A259   Chicago Cardinals (He and Linden Crow came to New York for Dick Nolan and Bobby Joe Conrad)

A260   Roosevelt Grier

A261   Dick James and Andy Stynchula

A262   He is the last number one pick who did not play with the team

TRADES, WAIVES, AND ACQUISITIONS

Q263   In the 1965 draft, the Giants passed on Joe Namath, Gale Sayers, Craig Morton, Dick Butkus, and John Huarte to choose this player. Name the running back.

Q264   All-Pro defensive end Fred Dryer had a distinguished career with the Rams but was originally drafted by the Giants. He played three seasons in New York before the team traded him in 1972. What was involved in the transaction?

Q265   New York and Denver swapped quarterbacks in 1977. Name the two players.

Q266   The Giants' number one pick in 1982, Butch Woolfolk, led the club in rushing during the 1982 and 1983 seasons. New York traded Woolfolk in the middle of the 1984 season. Where did he go, and who was involved in the transaction?

Q267   To what team was cornerback Mark Haynes traded in 1986?

Q268   Pepper Johnson and Ron Brown were both selected with 1986 draft choices acquired through a trade. What player did New York give up for those picks?

Q269   Ottis Anderson was acquired by New York from the Cardinals during the 1986 season. What two draft choices did the Giants give up for the running back?

Q270   Only two players on the Giants 1990 Super Bowl roster were acquired by trade. One was O. J. Anderson. Who is the other?

NEW YORK GIANTS

A263   Tucker Frederickson

A264   The Giants traded Dryer to New England for three draft choices; the Pats dealt him to the Rams for Rick Cash and a number one pick

A265   Craig Morton went to the Broncos for Steve Ramsey and future considerations (Ramsey never played for the Giants)

A266   Woolfolk was traded to Houston for a third-round pick in the 1985 draft.

A267   Denver Broncos (for draft choices)

A268   Mark Haynes (to Denver)

A269   A second- and seventh-round draft pick.

A270   LB Steve DeOssie (from dallas for a 1990 sixth-round draft pick.)

New York Jets

NEW YORK JETS

1968 NEW YORK JETS

Front Row, Left to Right TRAINER JEFF SNEDEKER, KARL HENKE, JIM RICHARDS, MIKE D'AMATO, HARVEY NAIRN, RANDY BEVERLY, BILL BAIRD, CORNELL GORDON, BILL RADEMACHER, GEORGE SAUER, HATCH ROSDAHL, ROBERT TAYLOR

Second Row, LARRY GRANTHAM, BAKE TURNER, DON MAYNARD, BILL MATHIS, CURLEY JOHNSON, RALPH BAKER, EARL CHRISTY, MIKE STROMBERG, TOMMY BURNETT, PAUL CRANE, AL ATKINSON, JEFF RICHARDSON, JOE NAMATH, HEAD COACH WEEB EWBANK.

Third Row, COACH CLIVE RUSH, EQUIPMENT MANAGER BILL HAMPTON COACH WALT MICHAELS, PETE LAMMONS, MARK SMOLINSKI, VERNON BIGGS, LEE WHITE, JIM TURNER, JIM HUDSON, JOHN SAMPLE, PAUL ROCHESTER, EMERSON BOOZER, MATT SNELL, TONY DiMIDIO, COACH JOE SPENCER, COACH BUDDY RYAN.

Fourth Row, CARL McADAMS, JOHN ELLIOTT, RAY HAYES, SAM WALTON, WINSTON HILL, JOHN SCHMITT, STEVE THOMPSON, RANDY RASMUSSEN, BOB TALAMINI, DAVE HERMAN, BABE PARILLI, GERRY PHILBIN.

THE SUITS

Q1 How many head coaches have the Jets had?

Q2 Who is the only New York coach with a career winning record (with the Jets)?

Q3 When did Sonny Werblin purchase the bankrupt New York Titans?

Q4 What two head coaches left the Jets in mid-season?

Q5 What two coaches attended Hardin-Simmons University?

Q6 Who was the former Penn football coach who served as the team's first general manager?

Q7 Who was the team's first coach?

Q8 What is Weeb Ewbank's given name?

Q9 What was Weeb Ewbank's record with the Colts in 1962, the year he was fired?

Q10 What did Weeb Ewbank accomplish as a coach that can never be duplicated?

Q11 Who succeeded Weeb Ewbank as the Jets' general manager in 1975?

Q12 Charley Winner was selected by Weeb Ewbank to replace him as head coach in 1974. How are the two men related?

Q13 Charley Winner was fired as head coach after a 7–7 record in 1974 and a 2–7 record in 1975. Who completed the 1975 season?

Q14 Lou Holtz left the Jets with one game left in the 1976 season to become a college head coach. At what school did he assume the position?

Q15 Who coached the Jets in the final game of the 1976 season?

Q16 Walt Michaels was voted the 1978 NFL Coach of the Year. What was the team's record that season?

NEW YORK JETS

A1   Ten

A2   No Jet coach has a winning record (Sammy Baugh has the best overall record, 14–14–0)

A3   1963

A4   Charley Winner (1975) and Lou Holtz (1976)

A5   Sammy Baugh and Bulldog Turner

A6   Steve Sabo

A7   Sammy Baugh (1960–61)

A8   Wilbur

A9   7–7

A10   Ewbank was the only coach to win world championships in both the NFL and the AFL.

A11   Al Ward

A12   Winner is Ewbank's son-in-law

A13   Offensive coordinator Ken Shipp

A14   Arkansas

A15   Mike Holovak

A16   8–8

Q17 In what capacity did Joe Walton serve with the Jets before he was named head coach of the team in 1983?

Q18 With what two NFL teams did Joe Walton play pro football?

Q19 How long was Bruce Coslet's coaching tenure in Cincinnati?

Q20 At 43, is Bruce Coslet the youngest head coach in the NFL?

Q21 What position did Coslet play in his eight-year pro career?

Q22 For what CFL team did Coslet play in 1968?

Q23 Who coached Bruce Coslet in seven of his eight seasons with the Cincinnati Bengals?

F.Y.I.

Q24 Whom did the Titans meet in their first pro football game?

Q25 Who scored the first touchdown in franchise history?

Q26 Who kicked the Jets' first PAT?

Q27 The first game the Titans played began on a sour note when the opening kickoff was returned 105 yards for a TD. Name the player who started the rout.

Q28 Against what team did New York register its first franchise victory on September 4, 1960?

Q29 Name the three members of the Jets organization who have been inducted into the Hall of Fame.

Q30 By what nickname was the Jets' 1981 defense known?

Q31 The Jets, as well as three other teams in the AFC's Eastern Division, play their home games on artificial turf. Name the only team in the division with a grass playing field.

NEW YORK JETS

A17   Offensive coordinator (1981–82)

A18   The Washington Redskins (1957–60) and the New York Giants (1961–63)

A19   Eight years (1981–89)

A20   No (he is three and a half months older than Art Shell)

A21   Tight end (Cincinnati: 1969–76)

A22   Edmonton (he was released after one season)

A23   Bill Walsh

------------------------ · ------------------------

A24   The Los Angeles Chargers (at the Coliseum; New York lost, 27–7, on August 6, 1960)

A25   Dick Jamieson (August 6, 1960: six-yard TD run)

A26   Bill Shockley (August 6, 1960)

A27   Charger Paul Lowe

A28   Buffalo Bills (a 52–31 preseason victory at Buffalo)

A29   Head coach Weeb Ewbank, Joe Namath, and Don Maynard

A30   New York Sack Exchange (the Jets had a league-leading 66 sacks)

A31   Miami Dolphins (Joe Robbie Stadium)

Q32   What were the Titans' team colors?

Q33   In what year did the franchise change its name from Titans to Jets?

Q34   In what year did the Jets adopt their present logo and uniform?

Q35   What did the AFL do for the Jets (and the Raiders) in 1963 in order to make them more competitive with the rest of the league?

Q36   When did the New York AFL franchise first register a winning season?

Q37   New York was the first two teams to appear on *Monday Night Football.* Whom did the Jets meet on September 21, 1970?

Q38   The first regular-season match-up between Gotham's two football teams took place on November 1, 1970. Who won?

Q39   O. J. Simpson broke the NFL's single-season rushing mark, becoming the first player to gain more than 2,000 yards in a game against New York. Of what significance was this 1973 game to the Jets' organization?

Q40   What world leader came to a Jets game in 1975 and watched New York defeat the Patriots, 36–7?

Q41   The first Monday night game in New York took place on October 15, 1979. What team did the Jets defeat that evening?

Q42   In the 4–12 1980 season, the Jets defeated only one team from the AFC's Eastern Division. Name the club.

Q43   Who was the Jets' final opponent in Shea Stadium?

Q44   The *Heidi Bowl*: NBC took it on the chin in 1968 as the Raiders scored two TDs in the last 65 seconds after the network cut away from the game so they could broadcast the children's classic. Who scored for the Raiders?

Q45   What was the final score in the *Heidi Bowl*?

Q46   In what year did the Jets move to Giants Stadium?

NEW YORK JETS

A32   Blue and gold

A33   1963

A34   1978

A35   It allowed the teams to select players from the other franchises

A36   1967 (8–5–1)

A37   Cleveland Browns (the Browns won, 31–21)

A38   Giants (22–10, at Shea)

A39   It was Weeb Ewbank's last game as head coach

A40   Emperor Hirohito of Japan

A41   Minnesota Vikings (14–7)

A42   Miami Dolphins (New York beat them twice in 1980)

A43   Pittsburgh Steelers (Steelers won, 34–7)

A44   Charlie Smith and Preston Ridlehuber

A45   Raiders over the Jets, 43–32

A46   1984

Q47 Who was the Jets' first opponent at Giants Stadium?

Q48 New York was the last team to play a game before the 1987 players' strike. Whom did they meet on that Monday, September 22?

Q49 The Jets' Monday night contest on October 9, 1989, was a momentous game in NFL history. What is its significance?

THE UNIFORMS

Q50 Who was the Jet who led the AFL in average yards per kickoff return in the league's inaugural (1960) season?

Q51 Name the player who was the first to see action with the Titans, Jets, and Giants.

Q52 What five Jets played in every AFL season from 1960 through 1969?

Q53 The Jets had two prized rookie quarterbacks in 1965: Namath and John Huarte. In what round and from what college was Huarte chosen?

Q54 Not including his two seasons with the Jets (1968 and 1969), with what AFL teams did Babe Parilli play?

Q55 Who was the backup QB behind Joe Namath in the 1975 season?

Q56 Who was the starting Jet QB in the 1979 season opener?

Q57 Name the two starting quarterbacks who played in the three replacement games during the 1987 season.

Q58 QB Kyle Mackey joined an AFC team during the 1987 replacement games and had his best outing as a pro against the Jets. For what team did he play?

Q59 Ken O'Brien threw 211 consecutive passes without an interception in the 1987 and 1988 seasons. What Detroit safety ended the second-longest streak in NFL history?

NEW YORK JETS

A47 Pittsburgh Steelers (Pittsburgh won, 23–17)

A48 New England (New York won, 43–24)

A49 The game marked the debut of Art Shell, the first black head coach in the NFL's modern era (the Raiders won, 14–7)

─────────────── · ───────────────

A50 Leon Burton (31 returns, 891 yards, 28.7 yards average per return, two TDs)

A51 Don Maynard

A52 Larry Grantham, Bill Mathis, Paul Rochester, Don Maynard, Babe Parilli (two seasons with the Jets)

A53 Second round; Notre Dame (Huarte never played for the Jets)

A54 Oakland Raiders (1960) and Boston Patriots (1961–67)

A55 J. J. Jones

A56 Matt Robinson

A57 David Norrie and Pat Ryan

A58 Miami Dolphins

A59 Raphael Cherry (September 25, 1988)

THE UNIFORMS

Q60 Who is the only quarterback from the class of 1983 to have a higher career passing rating than Ken O'Brien?

Q61 Who is the only Jet to lead the NFL in rushing yardage?

Q62 Name the two Jets who have led the league in receptions for a season.

Q63 Who led the Titans with 14 TD receptions in 1960?

Q64 In the team's first season, the Titans had two receivers with over 1,000 yards in receptions. Name the tandem.

Q65 What 1964 Jet led the AFL in interceptions?

Q66 What receiver signed with the Jets instead of the 49ers because Howard Cosell recommended the New York team?

Q67 Name the 1967 receivers who finished one-two in the AFL for receptions.

Q68 What Jet receiver quit pro ball in 1971 to launch a writing career?

Q69 Whom did Rich Caster replace as the starting tight end?

Q70 The Jets signed Jo Jo Townsell in 1985 after he had played three seasons in the USFL. For what team did he play in the rival league?

Q71 New York scored a 51–45 overtime win against Miami in 1986. Who caught the winning pass at the 2:35 mark of OT?

Q72 Name the Jet receiver who played running back behind Marcus Allen as a sophomore at UCLA.

Q73 This halfback led the team in rushing with only 431 yards—the least ever for the club's leading rusher. Who is this 1960 Jet?

Q74 Despite a disability, Wesley Walker established himself as one of the Jets' finest receivers. What handicap did he overcome?

Q75 Name the four players who comprised the New York Sack Exchange.

NEW YORK JETS

A60 Dan Marino

A61 Freeman McNeil (1982: 786 yards)

A62 George Sauer (1967: 75 receptions) and Al Toon (1988: 93 receptions)

A63 Art Powell

A64 Don Maynard (1,265 yards) and Art Powell (1,167 yards)

A65 Dainard Paulson (12 interceptions)

A66 Bob Schweickert

A67 George Sauer (75) and Don Maynard (71)

A68 George Sauer (he played five years with the Jets)

A69 Pete Lammons

A70 The L.A. Express

A71 Wesley Walker (he caught a 43-yard bomb from Ken O'Brien)

A72 Michael Harper

A73 Dewey Bohling (1960: 123 attempts, 431 yards, 3.5 average, two TDs)

A74 He is blind in one eye

A75 Mark Gastineau, Joe Klecko, Marty Lyons, and Abdul Salaam

Q76 Who was the first player to leave the Sack Exchange?

Q77 Who led the Jets and the league in sacks for the 1981 season?

Q78 How many times was Mark Gastineau named to the Pro Bowl?

Q79 Despite a near-record passing day by Dan Marino (521 yards), the Jets defeated Miami 44–30 in a 1988 game. Name the three New York defensive players who combined for five interceptions during the game.

Q80 Name the Jet who led the league for three seasons in yards gained in kickoff returns.

Q81 What other position did kicker Jim Turner play for New York?

Q82 Jim Turner kicked one or more field goals in 28 consecutive games (1970–72). Name the only player who exceeded that mark.

Q83 Jim Turner kicked 221 consecutive PATs during his career. Who is the only player to have booted more?

Q84 What punter failed to make the Jets in 1979 but hooked up with the Kansas City Chiefs and led the NFL in punting?

Q85 The Jets signed Pat Leahy in mid-1974 when their regular kicker went down with an injury. Whom did Leahy replace?

Q86 Name the four Jets who have been selected as the MVP in a Pro Bowl game.

Q87 What three Jets made the Pro Bowl (including the AFL All-Star Game) in their first two years in the league?

Q88 This Jet was the only defensive player in league history to appear in the Pro Bowl at three different positions. Name the player and the positions.

Q89 Name the six players from the Jets' Super Bowl team who made the 1969 All-Star squad.

Q90 What three Jets were named to the All-AFL team in 1969?

NEW YORK JETS

A76   Abdul Salaam (he was traded to San Diego in 1984)

A77   Joe Klecko (20½ sacks; Mark Gastineau had 20 sacks and was second in the league)

A78   Five times (1981–85)

A79   Carl Howard, Rich Miano, and Erik McMillan (3)

A80   Bruce Harper (1977–79)

A81   Quarterback (in a 1967 game against Miami, Turner was two for four and had 25 yards in passing; that was his only appearance as QB)

A82   Fred Cox (31 straight games)

A83   Tommy Davis of San Francisco (1959–65: 234)

A84   Bob Grupp

A85   Bobby Howfield

A86   Joe Namath (1966, 1968), Verlon Biggs (1967), Don Maynard (1968—co-recipient with Namath), and Mark Gastineau (1985)

A87   Billy Atkins, Billy Mathis, and Erik McMillan

A88   Joe Klecko; end, tackle, and nose tackle

A89   George Sauer, Pete Lammons, Joe Namath, Don Maynard, Verlon Biggs, and Larry Grantham

A90   Joe Namath, Don Maynard, and Gerry Philbin (Weeb Ewbank was named the all-time coach of the AFL)

THE UNIFORMS

Q91 Who was the first Jet to start in an NFL Pro Bowl?

Q92 Name the Jet who was a 1984 All-Pro selection as a kickoff returner.

Q93 Name the only Jet who was selected team MVP for three consecutive seasons by his teammates.

Q94 Who was the first Jet rookie since Emerson Boozer (1966) chosen for the Pro Bowl?

Q95 What was Abdul Salaam's name when he joined the team in 1976?

Q96 Name the coach who drafted and cut Winston Hill four months before the All-Star tackle joined the Jets in 1963.

Q97 At the end of the 1990 season, only two players had rushed for more yardage than Freeman McNeil among active rushers in the AFC. Who are they?

Q98 What Jet was invited to audition for the American Ballet Theater?

Q99 Five Turners have played with the Jets. Match each with his position.

(a) Rocky	(1) Defensive back
(b) Bake	(2) Kicker/QB
(c) Vince	(3) Receiver/safety
(d) Jim	(4) Running back
(e) Maurice	(5) Receiver

—BROADWAY JOE—

Q100 A few years before Namath was dubbed Broadway Joe, another Big Apple jock was known by the nickname. Who was the first Broadway Joe?

Q101 What major league club attempted to sign Namath to a baseball contract in 1961?

Q102 In 1963, Joe Namath missed the last two games of the season and the Sugar Bowl. Why was he out?

NEW YORK JETS

A91 Winston Hill (1972)

A92 Bobby Humphrey

A93 Al Toon (1986–88)

A94 Erik McMillan (1988)

A95 Larry Faulk

A96 Weeb Ewbank (while coaching Baltimore)

A97 Colt Eric Dickerson and Raider Marcus Allen

A98 Al Toon

A99 (a)—3; (b)—5; (c)—1; (d)—2; (e)—4.

------------------------ · ------------------------

A100 Joe Pepitone (Yankee first baseman 1962–69)

A101 The Chicago Cubs

A102 Bear Bryant suspended him "for an infraction of training rules" (he was seen with an alcoholic drink)

Q103 The most significant trade in team history took place in 1964 when the Jets dealt the rights of a quarterback to Houston for a number one draft choice. The pick was used to select Namath in 1965. Name the player New York gave up.

Q104 Joe Namath's Alabama team lost the 1965 Orange Bowl, 21–17, to Texas. Name the three Longhorns and future Jets who contributed to the Crimson's defeat.

Q105 What NFL team drafted Namath with its first-round pick in 1965?

Q106 What uniform item distinguished Joe Willie from his teammates?

Q107 Namath did not start his first NFL game because Weeb Ewbank thought he was too inexperienced. Who opened at QB against the Houston Oilers?

Q108 Who caught the first regular-season pass thrown by Namath?

Q109 Joe Namath won Rookie of the Year honors in 1965 and became the third QB to capture the award (until then). Who were the other two?

Q110 Broadway Joe became the first QB to throw for more than 4,000 yards in the regular season when he passed for 4,007 in 1967. Whose single-season yardage record did Namath eclipse?

Q111 In 1972, Namath became the highest-paid player in the NFL. What was his annual salary?

Q112 Namath's single-game record for passing yardage was 496 yards on September 24, 1972. Whom was New York playing that day?

Q113 What WFL team tried to lure Namath away from the Jets with a hefty contract in 1975?

Q114 Who was the last Jet on the receiving end of a Namath touchdown pass?

Q115 With what team did Joe Namath end his playing career?

Q116 Who caught the last pass Joe Namath threw in his career?

NEW YORK JETS

A103   Jerry Rhome (he never played with Houston)

A104   Jim Hudson threw the winning TD to George Sauer, and Pete Lammons intercepted two of Broadway Joe's passes (when Hudson joined the Jets, he was switched to defensive back)

A105   The St. Louis Cardinals

A106   His white football shoes (his teammates wore black)

A107   Mike Taliaferro

A108   Don Maynard (September 28, 1965: 18 yards; second game of the season, against Kansas City)

A109   Bob Waterfield and Otto Graham

A110   Philadelphia's Sonny Jurgenson's (1961: 3,723 yards)

A111 $250,000 per year

A112   Baltimore Colts

A113   Chicago Winds

A114   Jerome Barkum (11/21/76: 11-yard pass vs. New England; Pats won, 38–24)

A115   L.A. Rams (he signed with L.A. on May 12, 1977, after being waived by New York)

A116   Chicago safety Gary Fencik (October 10, 1977: quarterbacking the Rams on a Monday night game, Namath threw to Charley Young, but Fencik wrestled the ball out of his hands. The Bears won, 24–23.)

*** FAST FACTS ***

Jets Single-Season Records

Rushing: Freeman McNeil, 1,331 yards (1985)
Passing (yards): Joe Namath, 4,007 yards (1967)
Passing (TDs): Al Dorow (1960) and Joe Namath (1967), 26 TDs
Receiving (yards): Don Maynard, 1,434 (1967)
Receiving (number): Al Toon, 193 (1988)

Q68. This Jet quit pro football to launch a writing career. Name him.

NEW YORK JETS

Q124. What was the name of Joe Namath's television series?

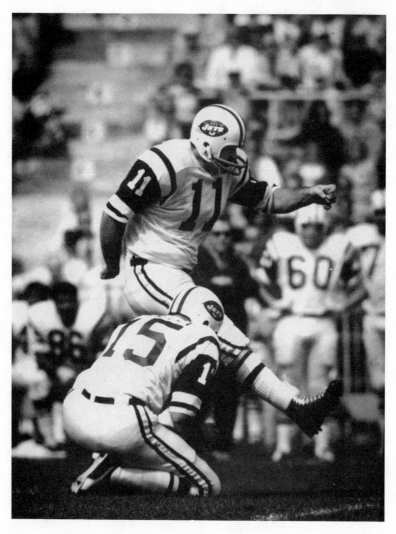

Q148. Jim Turner set a Super Bowl mark by attempting five field goals in one game. What kicker tied Turner's record in the 1978 Super Bowl?

Q208. Ken O'Brien was the fifth QB taken in the 1983 draft. Name the four quarterbacks taken ahead of him.

Q117 Name the last coach Namath played under.

Q118 How many 3,000-yard passing seasons did Broadway Joe have?

Q119 How many times was Namath pro football's leading passer (in terms of yardage)?

Q120 Namath set (and then twice tied) the team's single-game record for interceptions. How many did he toss?

Q121 Namath's record for aerial yardage stood for 12 seasons until another QB outdid him. Who cracked Namath's mark?

Q122 What were *Norwood* and *The Last Rebel?*

Q123 Who said, "I never want any of my kids to grow up like Joe Namath"?

Q124 What was the name of Joe Namath's television series?

—MAYNARD—

Q125 How many 1,000-yard seasons did Don Maynard have in his career?

Q126 With what team did Maynard play after the Giants released him in 1959?

Q127 Against what team did Don Maynard make his 632nd reception, making him pro football's all-time receiving leader?

Q128 After 15 years with the team, the Jets traded Maynard to the St. Louis Cardinals. What did they receive for the services of the Hall of Famer?

Q129 What receiving tandem was Don Maynard unable to beat out for a job in 1973, the year the Jets traded him to St. Louis?

Q130 After being released by the Cardinals and Rams in 1973, Maynard joined a World Football League team. Name the WFL team.

Q131 Don Maynard held the pro football record for reception yardage (11,834 yards) at the time of his retirement. Name the three receivers who have surpassed him.

NEW YORK JETS

A117 Chuck Knox

A118 Three (1966, 1967, and 1968)

A119 Three (1966: 3,379 yards; 1967: 4,007 yards; 1972: 2,816 yards)

A120 Six

A121 San Diego's Dan Fouts (1979: 4,082 yards)

A122 Joe Namath's first two movies

A123 Earl Morrall

A124 *The Waverly Wonders* (he played a high school basketball coach)

A125 Five (1960: 1,265 yards; 1962: 1,041 yards; 1965: 1,218 yards; 1967: 1,434 yards; 1968: 1,297 yards)

A126 The Hamilton Tiger Cats of the CFL

A127 Oakland Raiders (December 11, 1972: fourth quarter; Oakland won, 24–16)

A128 A draft choice

A129 Margene Adkins and David Knight

A130 Houston Texans (1974)

A131 Steve Largent (13,089 yards) and Charlie Joiner (12,146 yards), James Lofton (still active)

Q132 Whom did the Jets defeat in the 1968 AFL championship game?

Q133 With the Jets down 23–20 in the fourth quarter in the 1968 championship game, a Namath six-yard TD pass was the final score. Who was on the receiving end of the play?

Q134 The game was in doubt until the final moments, when a Daryl Lamonica lateral to Charlie Smith was fumbled and recovered by a Jet. Who jumped on the loose ball?

Q135 Who was the starting quarterback for the Colts in that game?

Q136 Who was the defensive captain on the Jets' Super Bowl team?

Q137 Super Bowl III matched the MVPs of the respective leagues against one another. Who were the 1968 NFL and AFL MVPs?

Q138 Name the four quarterbacks who played in Super Bowl III.

Q139 Who was the former Colt cornerback who called the coin toss (correctly) for the Jets in that contest?

Q140 On the Colts' first possession, they drove to the Jet 19-yard line but failed to score. Name the kicker who missed the chip shot.

Q141 The game might have ended differently if the Colts had been able to convert a turnover into the game's first score. What Jet fumbled on his own 12-yard line in the first quarter?

Q142 Who scored the Colts' only TD?

Q143 How many TD passes did Namath throw in Super Bowl III?

Q144 Name the Jet who recovered the Colts' only fumble.

Q145 Who was Super Bowl III's MVP?

Q146 True or false: The 23 points scored in Super Bowl III are the lowest total registered by two teams in the annual classic.

Q147 The record for highest average gain (minimum: 10 carries) was established in Super Bowl III. Who established the mark with a 10½-yard average?

NEW YORK JETS

———————————— · ————————————

A132 Oakland Raiders (27–23 in New York)

A133 Don Maynard

A134 Ralph Baker

A135 Earl Morrall

A136 Johnny Sample

A137 NFL: Earl Morrall; AFL: Joe Namath

A138 Jets: Namath and Babe Parilli; Colts: Earl Morrall and John Unitas

A139 Johnny Sample

A140 Lou Michaels

A141 George Sauer (three plays later, Morrall threw an interception to kill the scoring chance)

A142 Jerry Hill (one-yard run)

A143 None (New York's only TD came on a four-yard run by Matt Snell)

A144 Ralph Baker

A145 Joe Namath (17 for 28, 206 yards, 0 interceptions, 0 TDs)

A146 False—Super Bowl VII (Dolphins against Redskins) had only 21 points, and Super Bowl IX (Steelers against Vikings) had 22 points

A147 Baltimore's Tom Matte

Q148 Who tied Jim Turner's Super Bowl record of five field goals attempted in one game?

Q149 Name the four members of the Titans who played in Super Bowl III with the Jets.

Q150 Who was the last Jet from Super Bowl III to leave the team?

Q151 What team defeated the Jets in the 1969 AFL playoffs, almost a year after their stunning Super Bowl win?

Q152 Besides the Jets, what AFC Eastern Division teams made the 1981 playoffs?

Q153 The Jets' first playoff victory in 1982 was a 44–17 win over the Cincinnati Bengals. What back rushed for 202 yards and scored a touchdown?

Q154 Name the free safety who returned an interception 98 yards for a TD against Cincinnati in that contest.

Q155 In the second round against the Raiders, the Jets staged a come-from-behind victory to post a 17–14 win. Who saved the day for New York with a pair of interceptions in the last 2:49?

Q156 The Jets were one step away from Super Bowl XVII when they met the Dolphins in Miami on January 23, 1983. What was the final score?

Q157 Only one offensive TD was made in the defensive battle of the 1982 championship game. Name the Dolphin who scored it.

Q158 In the 1985 AFC wild-card playoff, the Jets met the Patriots. What New England player knocked Ken O'Brien out of the game on the last play of the second half?

Q159 New England clinched the 26–14 victory when Johnny Rembert returned a fumbled kickoff 15 yards for a TD in that playoff. Who lost the handle on the play?

Q160 The Jets defeated Kansas City in the 1986 AFC wild-card playoff 35–15. Who swiped a Todd Blackledge pass in the second half and took it in for a touchdown?

NEW YORK JETS

A148 Dallas's Efren Herrera (1978: against Denver)

A149 Don Maynard, Larry Grantham, Bill Mathis, and Curley Johnson

A150 Randy Rasmussen (1967–81)

A151 Kansas City (13–6)

A152 Division winner Miami and wild-card qualifier Buffalo

A153 Freeman McNeil

A154 Darrol Ray

A155 Lance Mehl

A156 Miami won, 14–0

A157 Woody Bennett (A. J. Duhe scored the other on a 35-yard interception return)

A158 Andre Tippett (O'Brien played the first series of the second half before he gave way to Pat Ryan)

A159 Return man Johnny Hector

A160 Kevin McArthur (21-yard interception return)

GLORY DAYS

Q161 In the 1986 divisional playoff, the Jets met the Browns in Cleveland. What was the final score?

Q162 In the third-longest game in NFL history (77:02), Cleveland rallied to tie the game in the final 4:14 of regulation. How many points did they score in that time?

Q163 Who kicked the winning field goal in the 1986 AFC divisional playoff?

SETTING THE STANDARD

Q164 Who holds the Jets' iron man (consecutive-game) record?

Q165 Who has played the most games in a Jet uniform?

Q166 Who handed the Jets their worst defeat?

Q167 The Jets have led the league once in regular-season points scored. In what year did they achieve that mark?

Q168 Pat Leahy became the 13th player in NFL history to register 1,000 points in 1987. Who were the Jets playing when Leahy reached the plateau?

Q169 Whom did the Jets annihilate when they scored a club-high 62 points in a 1979 game?

Q170 Who is the only Jet quarterback to lead the NFL in passer ratings?

Q171 Ken O'Brien established an AFC record when he attempted 211 consecutive passes without an interception in the 1987 and 1988 seasons. Who holds the NFL record?

Q172 Who ended O'Brien's noninterception streak?

Q173 How many passes did Richard Todd complete in the September 21, 1980, game against San Francisco?

NEW YORK JETS

A161 23–20, Cleveland victory

A162 10 points

A163 Mark Mosely (27 yards)

--- · ---

A164 Winston Hill (1963–76: 195 games, including 174 straight starts)

A165 Pat Leahy (1974–89: 219 games)

A166 New England (1979: 56–3)

A167 1960 (the 382 points scored led the AFL and also topped the NFL's leading scoring team, the Cleveland Browns, by 20 points)

A168 The Buffalo Bills

A169 Tampa Bay (1985: Jets won, 62–28)

A170 Ken O'Brien (1985: 96.4)

A171 Bart Starr (1964–65: 294 passes)

A172 Detroit's Raphael Cherry

A173 42 (it was a new league record)

Q174 Name the two players who hooked up for the longest pass play in Jet history—96 yards against Buffalo.

Q175 Johnny Hector's 11 rushing TDs in 1987 equaled the club mark. Name the fleet-footed back who first set the record.

Q176 What two Jets were the first backs to rush for more than 150 yards in the same game?

Q177 Who was the Jets' first 1,000-yard rusher?

Q178 Who set the team record for rushing yards in a game?

Q179 While playing for Washington, John Riggins set a record for TDs scored in a season with 24. Who held the previous record of 23?

Q180 What Jet receiver caught a team-record 17 passes against the 49ers in 1980?

Q181 Name the Jet who set a team record for receptions in consecutive games.

Q182 Name the New York defensive back who established a team record by returning an interception 92 yards for a TD against Indianapolis.

Q183 In 1981, the Jets set a league record for sacks. How many times did they get to the opposing quarterback?

Q184 Name the Titan who tied an NFL record by returning two punts for touchdowns in a 1961 game.

Q185 Bruce Harper returned 243 kickoffs in his eight-year career with the Jets (1977–84). Who is the only player in league history to handle more kickoffs?

Q186 Jim Turner ranks third on the all-time scorers list with 1,439 points (one TD, 304 FGs, 521 PATs). What two players rank above him?

Q187 Jim Turner set a team record when he kicked six field goals in a game against Buffalo in 1968. Who tied his mark?

NEW YORK JETS

A174   Ken O'Brien to Wesley Walker (December 8, 1985)

A175   Emerson Boozer

A176   John Riggins (168 yards) and Emerson Boozer (150 yards) (October 15, 1972: against Patriots)

A177   John Riggins (1975: 1,005 yards)

A178   Freeman McNeil (1985: 192 yards)

A179   O. J. Simpson

A180   Clark Gaines (September 21, 1980)

A181   Mickey Shuler

A182   Erik McMillan (October 1, 1989)

A183   66 times

A184   Dick Christy (September 24, 1961: against Denver)

A185   Ron Smith (275 returns, 1965–74; five teams)

A186   George Blanda (2,002 points) and Jan Stenerud (1,699 points)

A187   Bobby Howfield (December 3, 1972: against New Orleans)

SETTING THE STANDARD

Q188   Who is the only Jet to kick two 50-plus-yard field goals in a single game?

Q189   The NFL record for field goals in a season was established by Jim Turner in 1968 when he kicked 34. The record stood for 15 seasons until this NFC kicker broke it. Name him.

Q190   What Jet holds the NFL record for the longest punt?

Q191   Ken O'Brien was sacked an NFL-record 62 times in 1985, but the mark was broken the next season. Who was sacked 72 times in 1986?

TRADES, WAIVES, AND ACQUISITIONS

Q192   Whom did the Jets select in the AFL's first draft of 1959?

Q193   Name the three Ohio State Buckeyes who were first-round draft picks of New York.

Q194   Name the four quarterbacks the Jets drafted in the first round.

Q195   Name the four fullbacks the Jets have selected in the first round.

Q196   What college has produced the most Jets?

Q197   Only two linebackers have been chosen by the Jets with their top draft pick. Who were they?

Q198   Who was the first player signed by the Titans in 1960?

Q199   In 1961, the Titans drafted second in the AFL and selected 27 players in 30 rounds. Who was the highest draft choice to play with New York?

Q200   In 1964, this player was the first-round draft choice of the Jets and the third-round pick of the Giants. Name him.

Q201   Whom did the Jets receive when they traded Mike Taliaferro to New England in 1968?

NEW YORK JETS

A188 Pat Leahy (October 20, 1985: vs. New England)

A189 Giant Ali Haji-Sheikh

A190 Steve O'Neal (September 21, 1969: 98 yards vs. Denver)

A191 Philadelphia's Randall Cunningham

A192 George Izo (the draft was by position; Izo, a QB, never played with the Jets)

A193 Matt Snell (1964), Dave Foley (1969), and Chris Ward (1978)

A194 Sandy Stephens (1962), Joe Namath (1965), Richard Todd (1976), and Ken O'Brien (1983)

A195 Matt Snell (1964), Lee White (1968), John Riggins (1971), and Roger Vick (1987)

A196 Penn State

A197 Bob Crable (1982) and Jeff Lageman (1989)

A198 Don Maynard

A199 Fullback Bob Brooks, the 21st pick, from Ohio State

A200 Matt Snell

A201 Babe Parilli

TRADES, WAIVES, AND ACQUISITIONS

Q202 In a straight-up deal involving kickers, what British native came to the Jets from Denver after Jim Turner was dispatched to the Broncos in 1971?

Q203 The Jets acquired a 1972 first-round pick from Washington for what defensive end?

Q204 To what team did New York trade their first pick in the 1975 draft?

Q205 Whom did the Jets gain in that 1975 trade?

Q206 In what round was Pat Ryan drafted in 1978?

Q207 To what team was Matt Robinson traded in 1980 for a first- and second-round pick and Craig Penrose?

Q208 Ken O'Brien was the fifth QB taken in the 1983 draft. Name the four quarterbacks selected ahead of him.

Q209 The quarterback controversy raged between Richard Todd and Pat Ryan until Todd was traded in 1984. To what team was he sent?

Q210 Bobby Humphrey was sent to the Rams for L.A.'s 1990 fifth-round draft pick. Whom did the Jets select with the choice?

NEW YORK JETS

A202   Bobby Howfield

A203   Verlon Biggs (New York selected Michigan linebacker Mike Taylor)

A204   New Orleans Saints

A205   Billy Newsome (1975–76)

A206   11th round (from Tennessee)

A207   Denver Broncos (he played one season with Denver before being released)

A208   John Elway (Colts), Todd Blackledge (Chiefs), Jim Kelly (Bills), Tony Eason (Patriots)

A209   New Orleans (for a first-round pick in the 1984 draft)

A210   Texas Christian defensive back Robert McWright

*** FAST FACTS ***

Jets Coaching History

	Regular Season			Playoffs	
	Won	Lost	Tied	Won	Lost
Sammy Baugh (1960–61)	14	14	0		
Clyde (Bulldog) Turner (1962)	5	9	0		
Weeb Ewbank (1963–73)	73	78	6	2	1
Charley Winner (1974–75)	9	14	0		
Ken Shipp (1975)	1	4	0		
Lou Holtz (1976)	3	10	0		
Mike Holovak (1976)	0	1	0		
Walt Michaels (1977–82)	41	49	1	2	2
Joe Walton (1983–89)	54	59	1	1	2
Bruce Coslet (1990–)	6	10	0		
Total	206	248	8	5	5

Bibliography

BIBLIOGRAPHY

Barzman, Sol. *505 Basketball Questions Your Friends Can't Answer.* New York: Bonanza Books, 1983.

Boucher, Frank, with Trent Frayne. *When the Rangers Were Young.* New York: Dodd, Mead, 1973.

Brase, Dave, and Tim Simmons. *The Sports Time Machine.* Milbrae, Calif.: Celestial Arts, 1974.

Carruth, Gordon, and Eugene Ehrlich. *Facts and Dates of American Sports.* New York: Harper & Row, 1988.

Clary, Jack. *Pro Football's Great Moments.* New York: Bonanza Books, 1983.

Creamer, Robert W. *Babe—The Legend Comes to Life.* New York: Simon & Schuster, 1974.

Frommer, Harvey. *New York City Baseball—The Last Golden Age: 1947–1957.* New York: Macmillan, 1980.

Gallagher, Mark. *Day by Day in New York Yankees History.* New York: Leisure Press, 1983.

Hernandez, Keith, and Mike Bryan. *If at First—A Season With the Mets.* New York: McGraw-Hill, 1986.

Hoppel, Joe. *The Sporting News Baseball Trivia Book.* St. Louis: Sporting News Publishing Co., 1983.

Kenville, Mark F. *N.Y. Jets Trivia.* Boston: Quinlan Press, 1986.

Kingston, John. *505 Baseball Questions Your Friends Can't Answer.* New York: Walker, 1980.

Langford, Walter M. *Legends of Baseball: An Oral History of the Game's Golden Age.* South Bend, Ind.: Diamond Communications, 1987.

LeConte, Walter. *The Ultimate New York Yankees Record Book.*

BIBLIOGRAPHY

New York: Leisure Press, 1984.

Libby, Bill. *Classic Contests of Sports.* New York: Hawthorn Books, 1974.

Martin, Billy, with Phil Pepe. *BillyBall.* Garden City, N.Y.: Doubleday, 1987.

Mercurio, John A. *Chronology of New York Yankee Records.* New York: Harper & Row, 1989.

1988–89 Guinness Sports Record Book. New York: Sterling, 1989.

Reichler, Joseph L. *The Great All-Time Baseball Record Book.* New York: Macmillan, 1981.

Snider, Duke, with Bill Gilbert. *The Duke of Flatbush.* New York: Kensington Publishing Corp., 1988.

Vickroy, Richard L., and Herbert A. Ruth. *The Ultimate Baseball Trivia Book.* Middle Village, N.Y.: Jonathan David, 1986.

Weil, Bob, and Jim Fitzgerald. *The Yankee Quizbook.* Garden City, N.Y.: Dolphin Books, 1981.

Whittingham, Richard, ed. *The Fireside Book of Football.* New York: Simon & Schuster, 1989.